## Dedicated to my Family:
## Yasuko, Yvonne, Kenji & Masaki

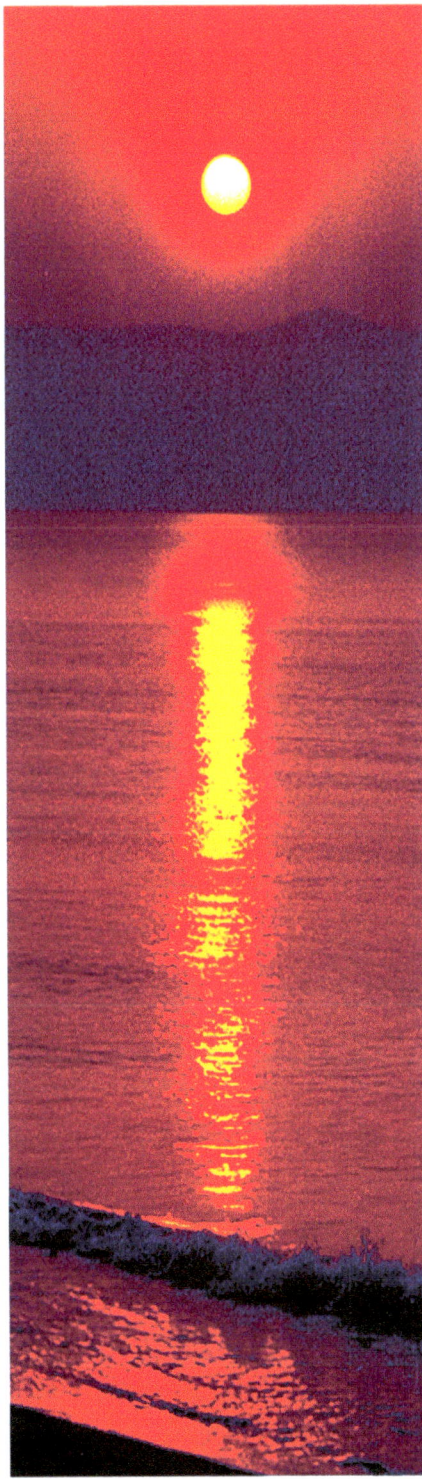

2nd Edition     2012

First published in 2010  by
Compass Films, 22 Chelverton Dr.
New Zealand, 0932

(Combining  Vol.1 & 2 of Assignment Earth)

Mitchell, Wayne
Assignment World    Photo Essays by Wayne Mitchell

ISBN    978-0-473-16928-2

1. Travel,  Experiences, Adventure,  Worldwide, Asia, Africa,
    South America, Latin America,  Tribes, Indians, Filming.

Copies may be ordered from
compfilm@clear.net.nz

Other titles by author:
The Umpteenth International SCARECROW Convention
The ByWAY Is MyWAY        Adventures worldwide
From Out of The Past       Part 1:  Myths & Legends
                                       Part 2:  Tall Tales Of The WEST

The Human Image  DVD   Art History
                                       from Neanderthal to Abstract

Tall Tales of The WEST  DVD     History & Humor

Zen simplicity.
A Mondrian-like composition of a Shinto shrine
at Miyajima, Japan.

From here, the priests saw what seemed to be the end
of the world, when a bomb was dropped on the
nearby city of Hiroshima, just across the channel.

2

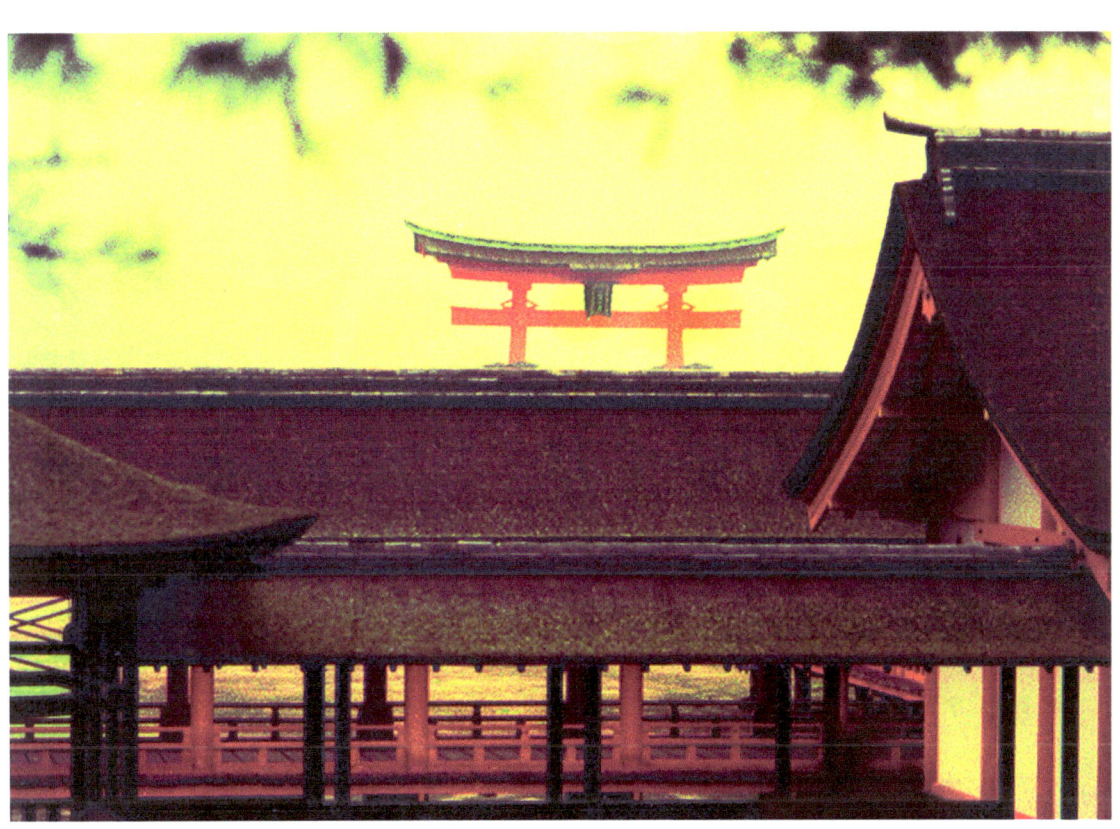

During the Barong dance in Bali, a group
of "assassins" attempt to kill the prince.

This is a story from the Hindu classic:
Ramayana.   As the assassins attack, a
majic spell is suddenly cast on them,
forcing their daggers to turn away from
the prince, and then the assassins become
victims ... attacked by their own daggers.

In spite of heavy tourism in Bali, the people have
maintained their traditions:  art, dance, religion,
music, and crafts, with little of the decline that
usually results from commercializing exotic
cultures.

Even the creftspeople from Java, who have been
lured to Bali by the tourist market, continue to
produce high quality batik cloth, woodcarvings,
and leather shadow puppets.

4

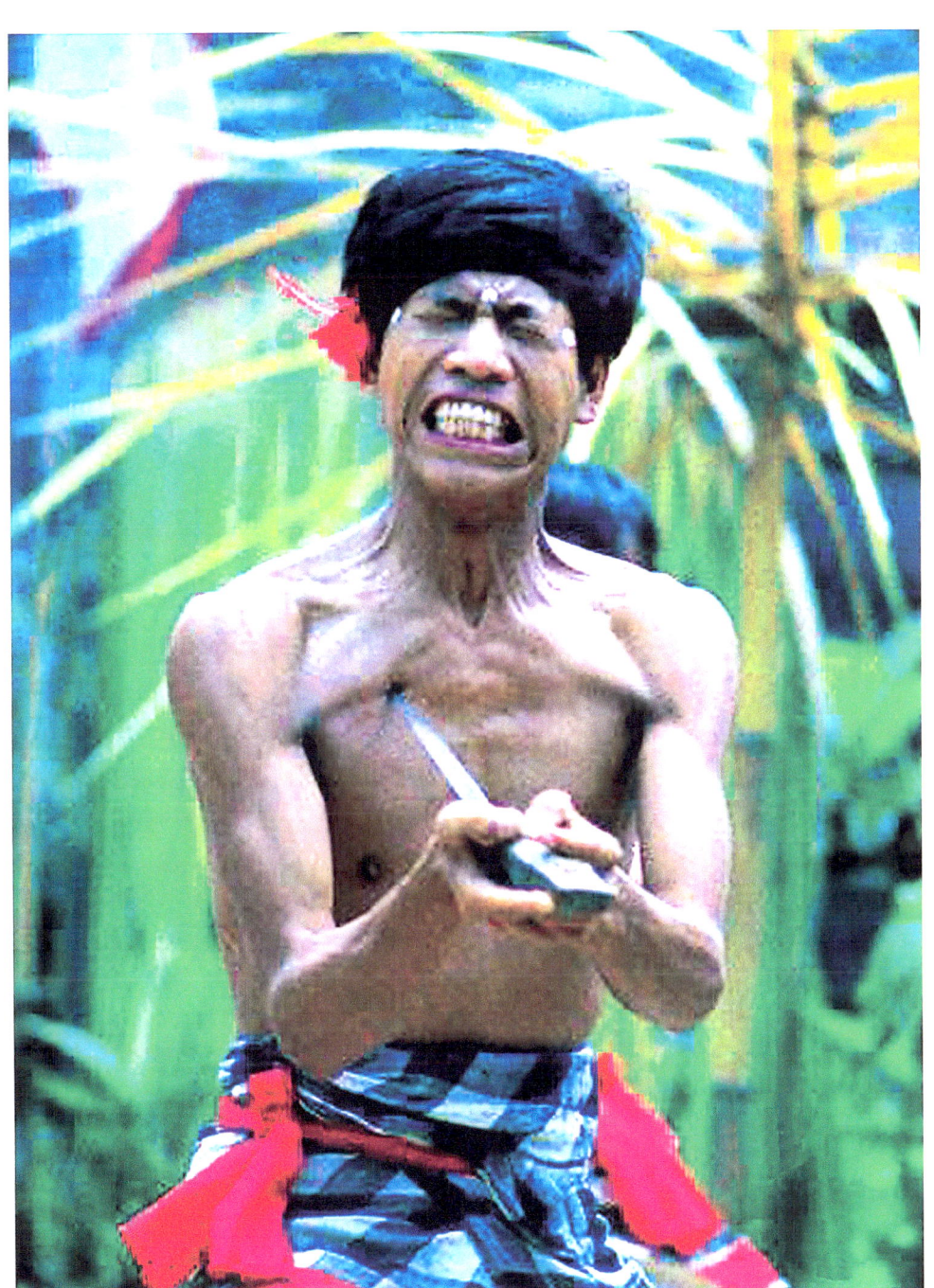

A mouthful of pearls.

This beachboy could actually be from any nation
or island around the Caribbean.  He's a descendant
of runaway slaves ... perhaps from Cuba Hispaniola.

These "Libres", now living along the coast of Beliz,
Honduras, Nicaragua, etc.  are somewhat ignored by
their governments,  so they've managed to keep a
stronger African heritage than so many of their
Caribbean cousins.

This youngster wanders among the beach tourists,
earning tips by singing both Calipso and Salsa to them.

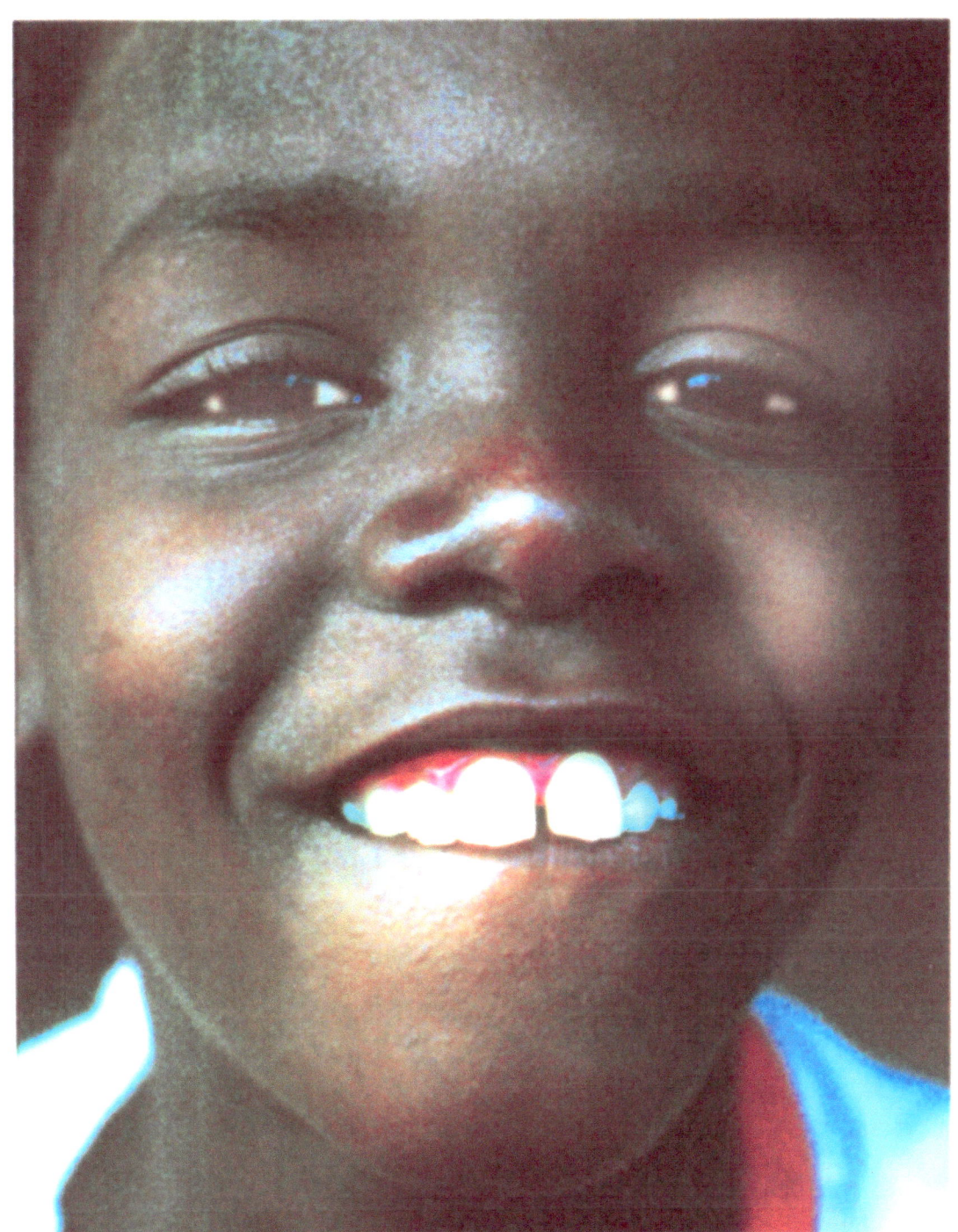

A symbol of Peace ...

this white dove rests at a mosque near the war-torn border of Afghganistan and Iran.  Surrounded by centuries-old glazed tiles, with geometric and floral designs, she is the only sign of life.

Moslim rules forbid the depiction of life in their art. Even the vases and flowers behind her are depicted as symbolic designs.

Beneath the mosque is a workshop, where one family has continued the tradition of many centuries, making exact copies of the tiles, to replace any that have cracked or fallen from the walls .

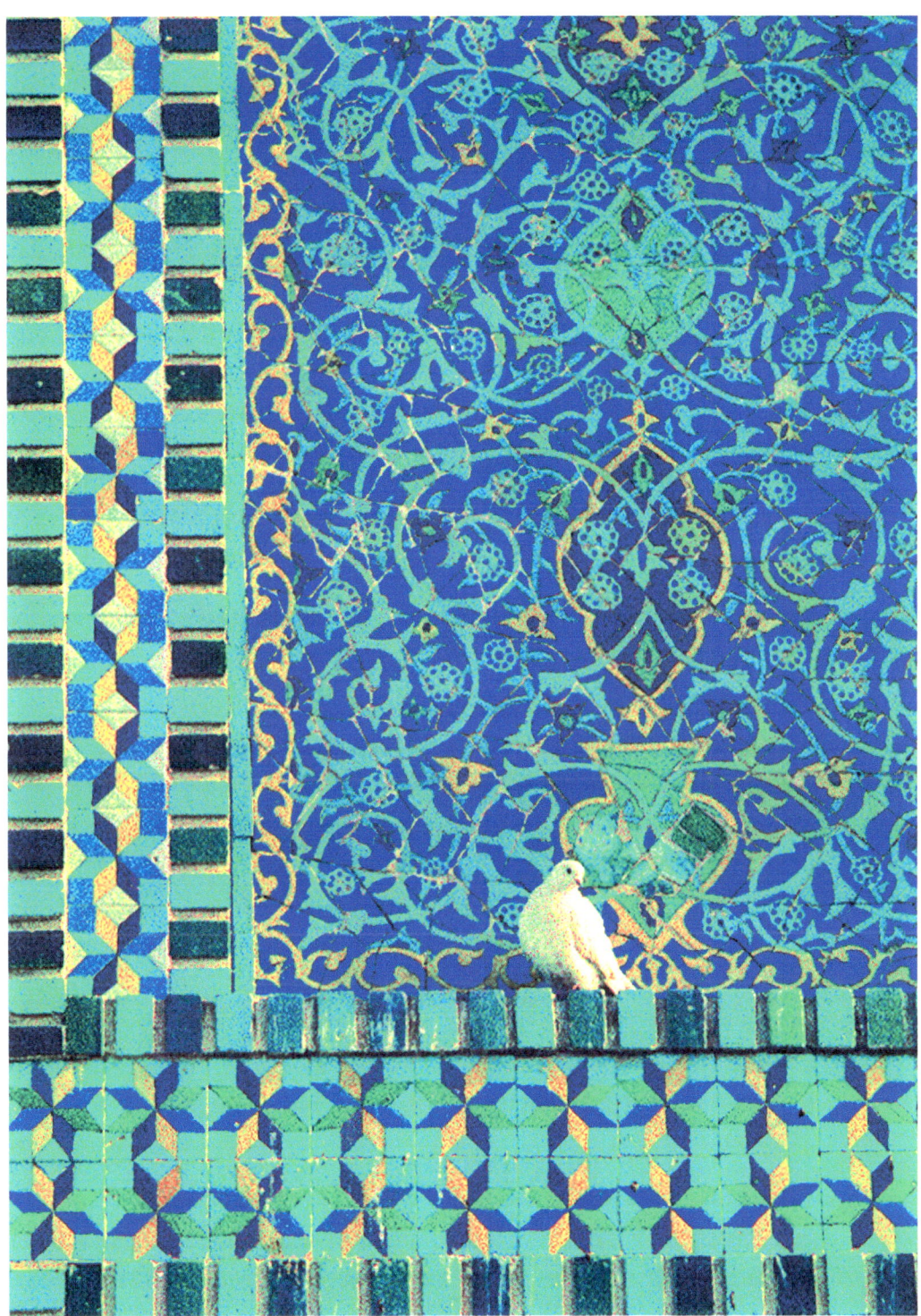

# Eskimo Maiden

On Nunivac Island, out in the Bering Sea,
live one of the most isolated tribes of
Alaskan Eskimo ... these are the Chup'ic,
whose life still centers around the hunting
of walrus and seal.

Sometimes the ice-pack around Nunivac
does not melt for several years in a row,
keeping the annual supply ship from
reaching them.  Today an airplane tries to
fly in whenever weather permits ...
bringing such necessities as soda-pop.

None of the Alaskan Eskimo tribes should
be called  "Inuit".  That is a tribal name for
those in Canada, and perhaps Greenland.

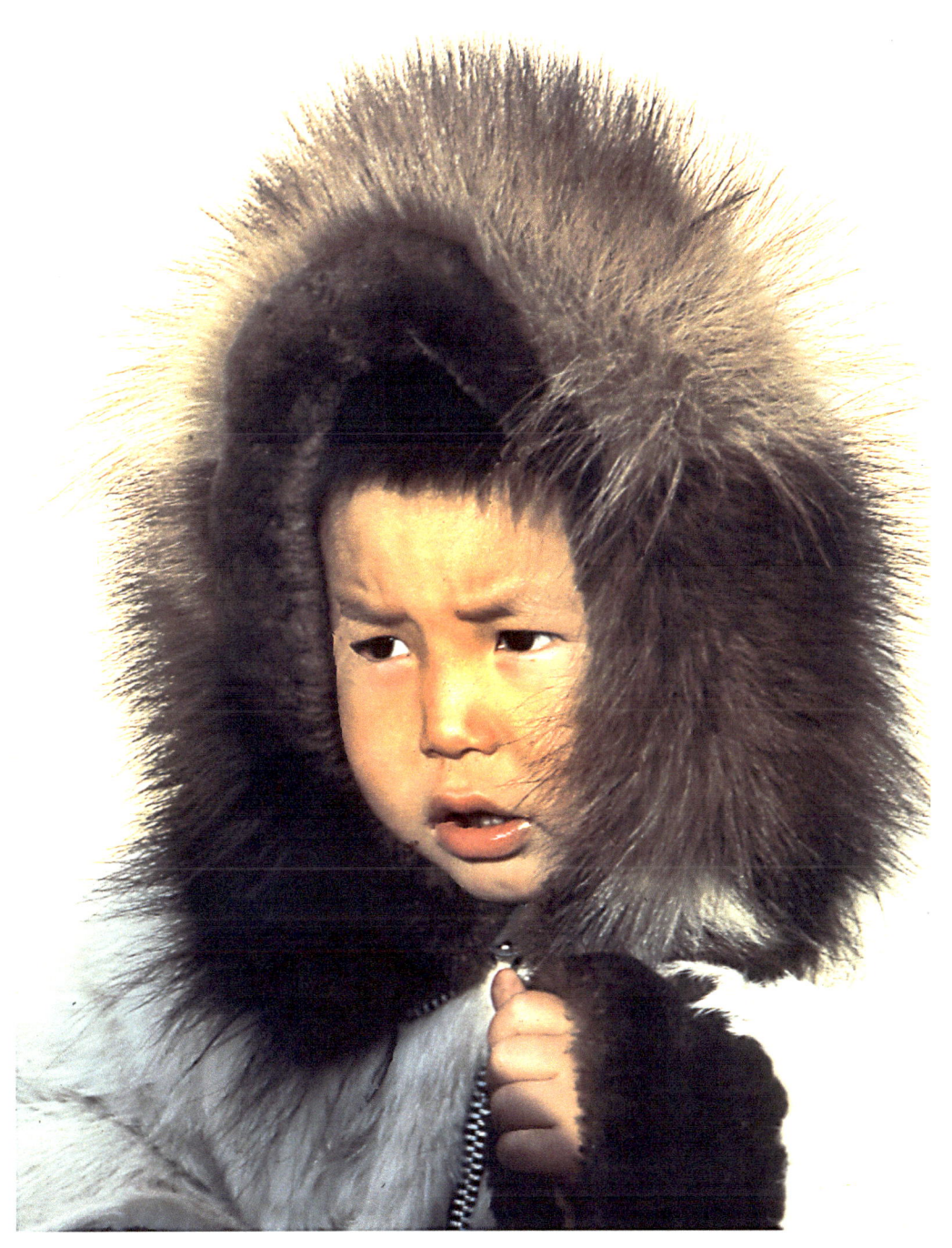

**Centuries ago
during Islam's expansion across much of
Western Asia and North Africa, their
skilled architects designed and built massive
Mosques … without power tools or modern
materials.
This is the  great Blue Mosque in war-torn
Herat, Afghanistan … still so beautiful …
its huge size making us feel insignificant …
impressing the thousands of worshipers
who come here every week to pray.**

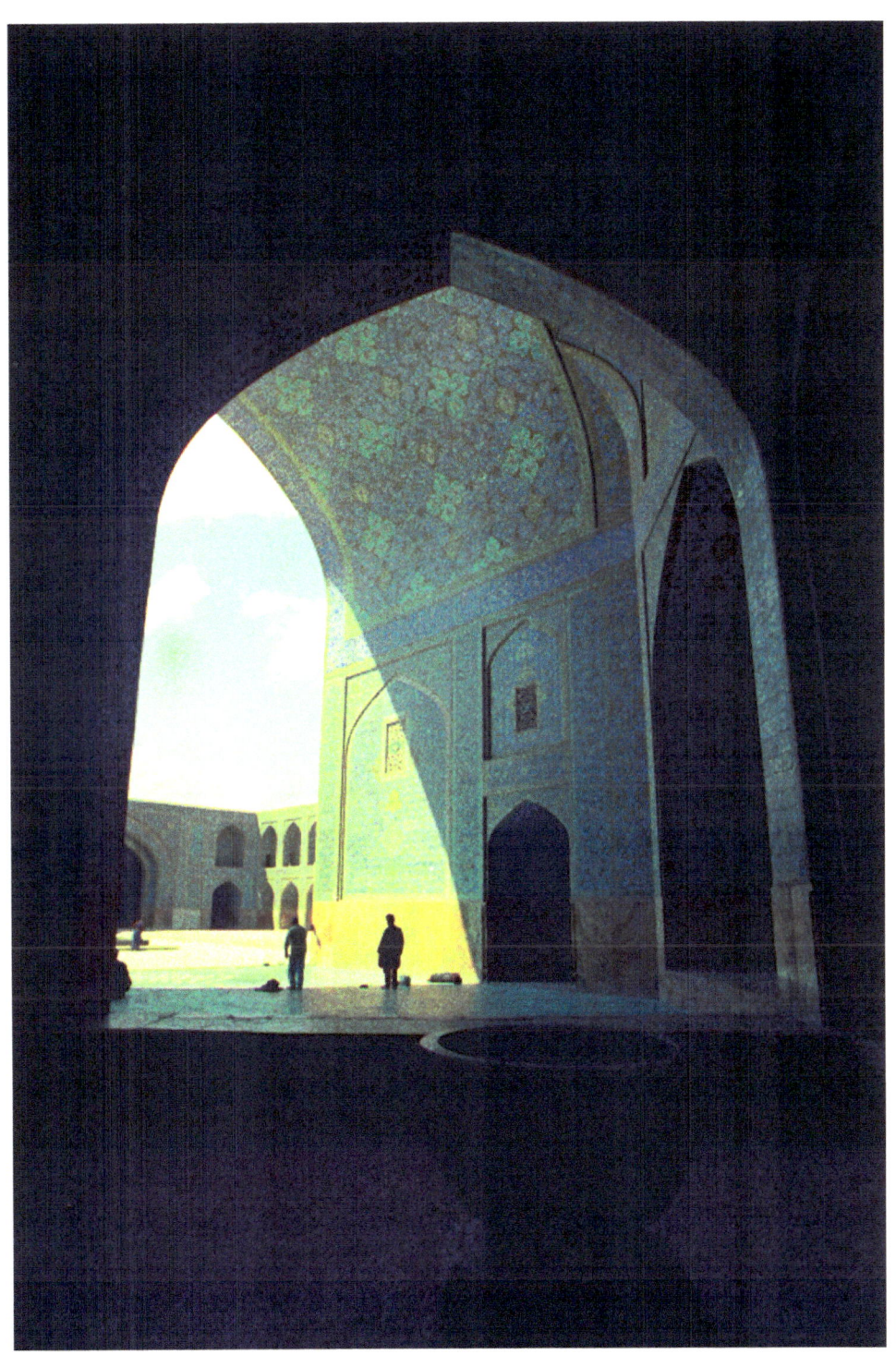

## "FUJI-LIPS"

Or should it be "Moon-Face" ?
Among the thousands gathered for the August
Bon Festival, in a village of northern Japan, *her*
face stands out, intensely watching the Odori
dancers ... perhaps wishing she was old enough
to join.

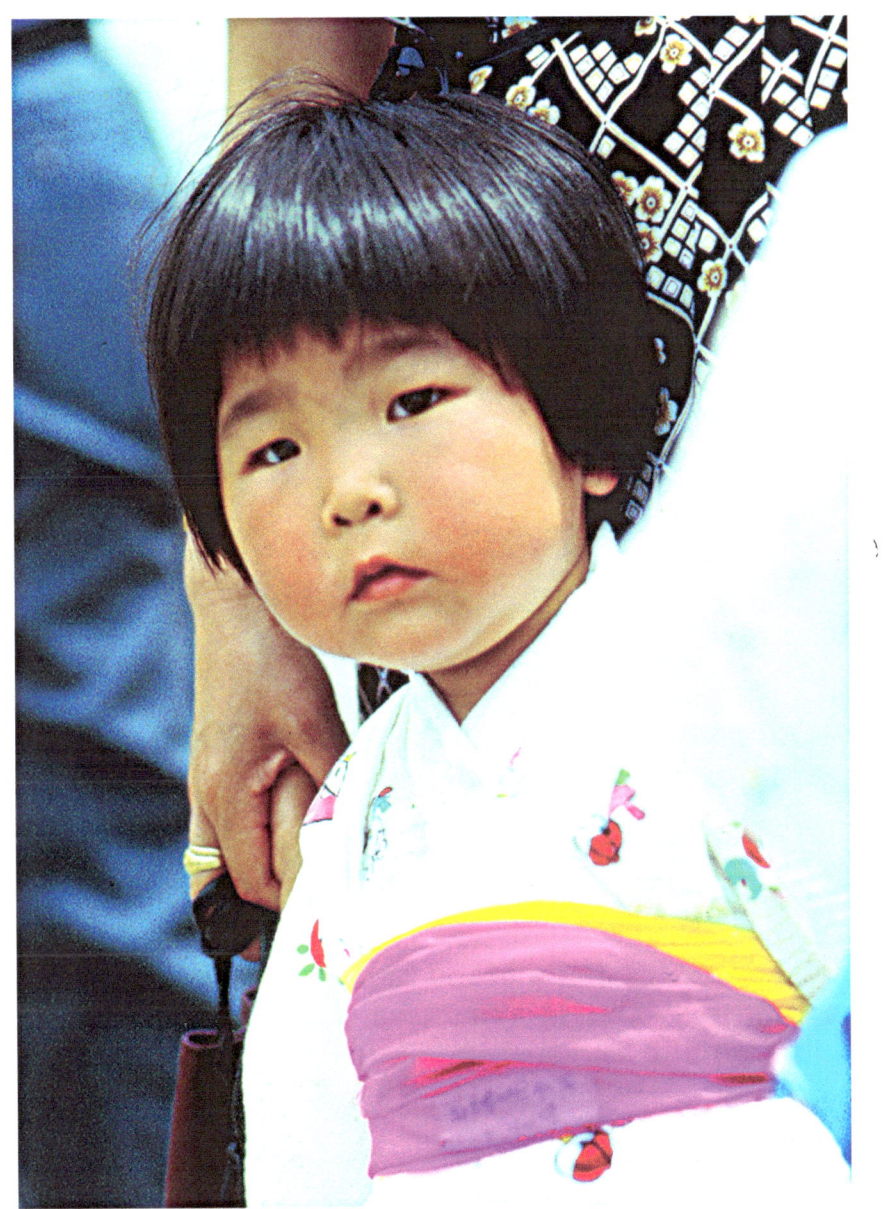

Orthodox Icon School

**Out on Paros Island, in the Adriatic Sea, this monastery has one of the last schools teaching the painting of traditional Christian icons.**

**Paros is famous in Greek mythology, and for its white marble which was quarried in ancient times for many of the famous Grecian sculptures. This monastery also still continues its tradition of never allowing a woman to set foot in it**

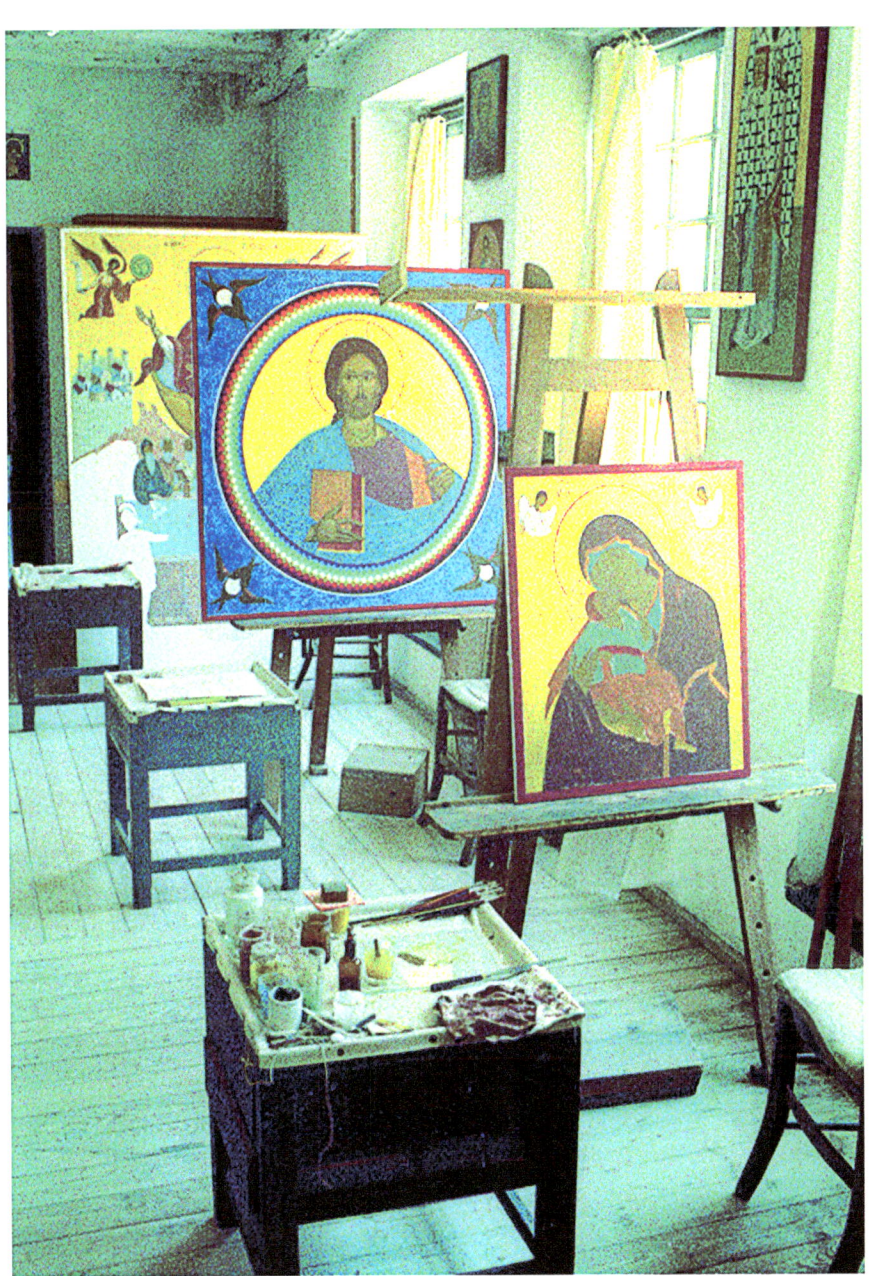

Not far from the Indus River,
in central Pakistan, this farmer was gracious as
a host, philosopher, and storyteller.  He had
found us setting up camp under one of his
roadside trees.  Claiming this was too
dangerous, he invited us to move into a room in
his large compound, and then have dinner with
his family.  He later insisted that we stay for
days, which we did, plus having discussions
about the world, the ancient Indus civilizations,
touring his fields, learning his traditional
farming techniques, and bathing under his
irrigation pumps.

Days later we accompanied him on a drive to the
city of Multan, to return his two teenage
daughters to their university.  But before leaving
the house, what a surprise to see these modern
outspoken girls cover themselves completely, in
traditional black chador veils,.  Until then we
had not realized they would never allow
themselves to be seen in public with only their
eyes showing through a lace slit.

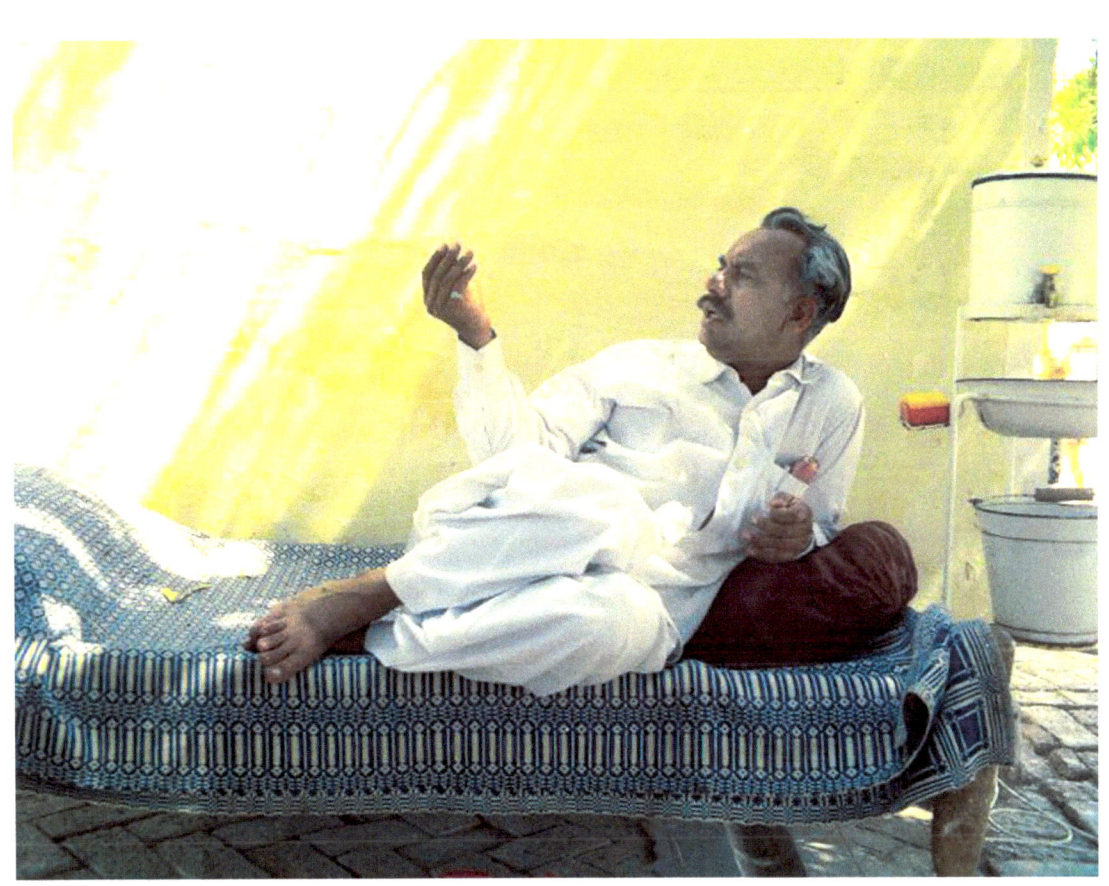

Near Katmandu, Nepal,

this towering crown, atop a Buddhist Stupa, is
decorated for a festival.  Buried far inside the
white domed stupa is a small container, holding
a few hairs, fingernails, or personal treasures
from the
Gautama Buddha, or one of his disciples.

20.

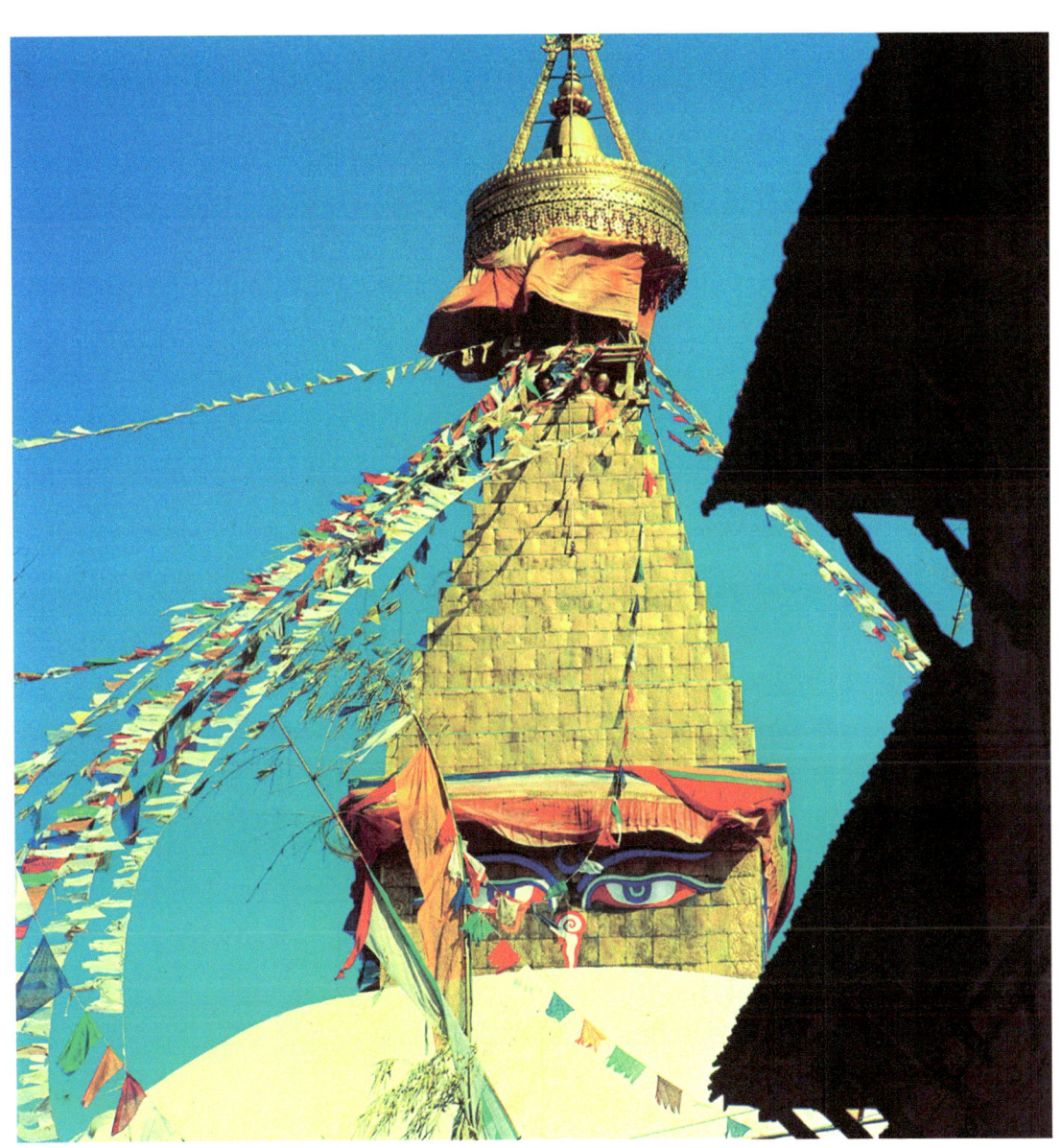

Henry Old Coyote Sr.
(1957)
Elder of the Crow tribe in Montana.
Raised his family to respect their ancient
traditions.  Sons Hank and Barney Old Coyote,
who served in World War Two, collected stories
of the old days from him and other elders.
Most of his children and grandchildren are
university graduates and teachers.  One of
them, Phenocia Bauerle, recently edited and
published a book of their old tribal stories:
"Way of The Warrior".

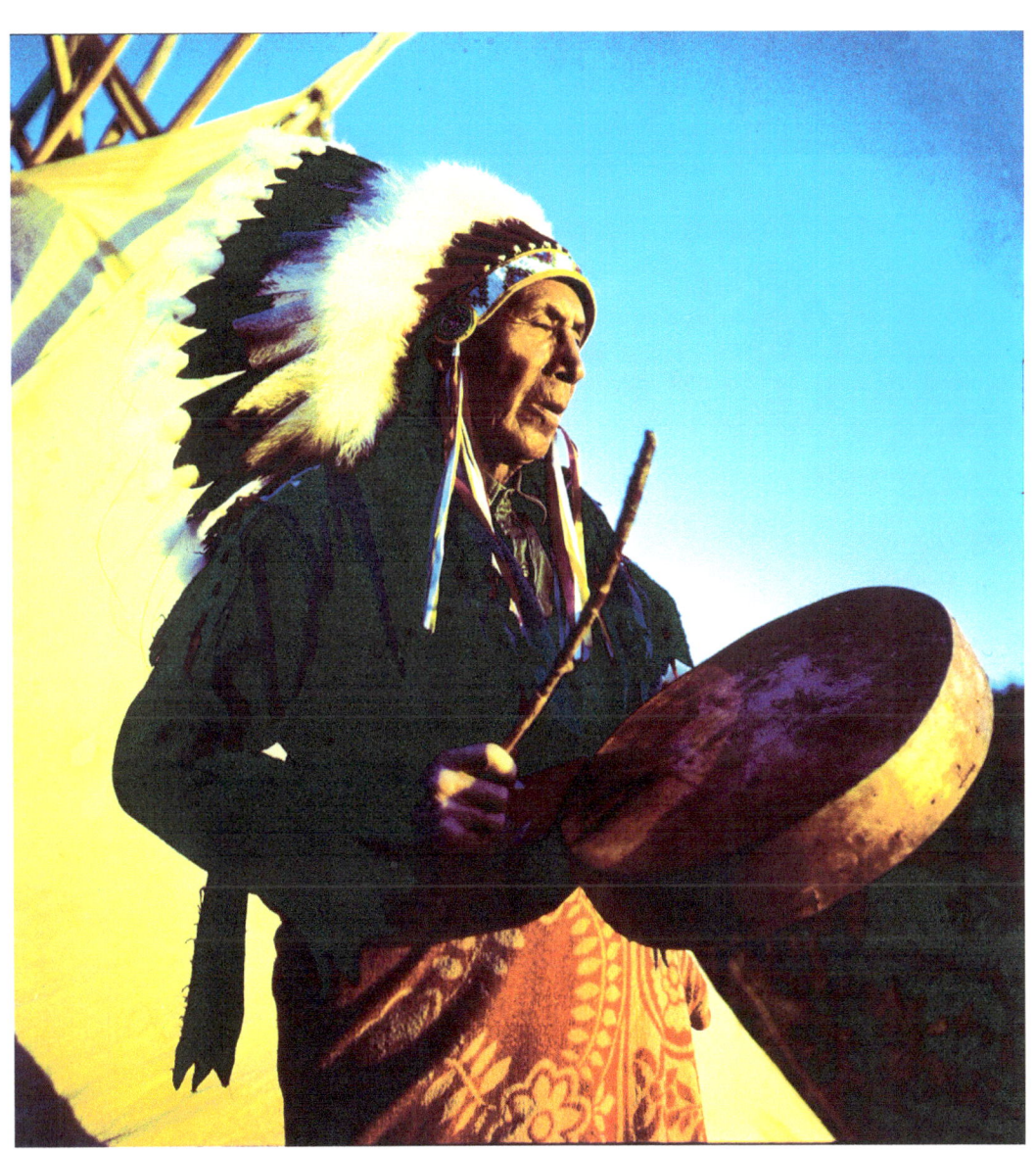

Traditional rural folk dance,

one of the many entertainments going on during
the late summer festivals held throughout Japan .
.
This one is at the famous Horse Festival held
near the coastal town of Soma, where the riders
dress in traditional Samurai warriors armor.

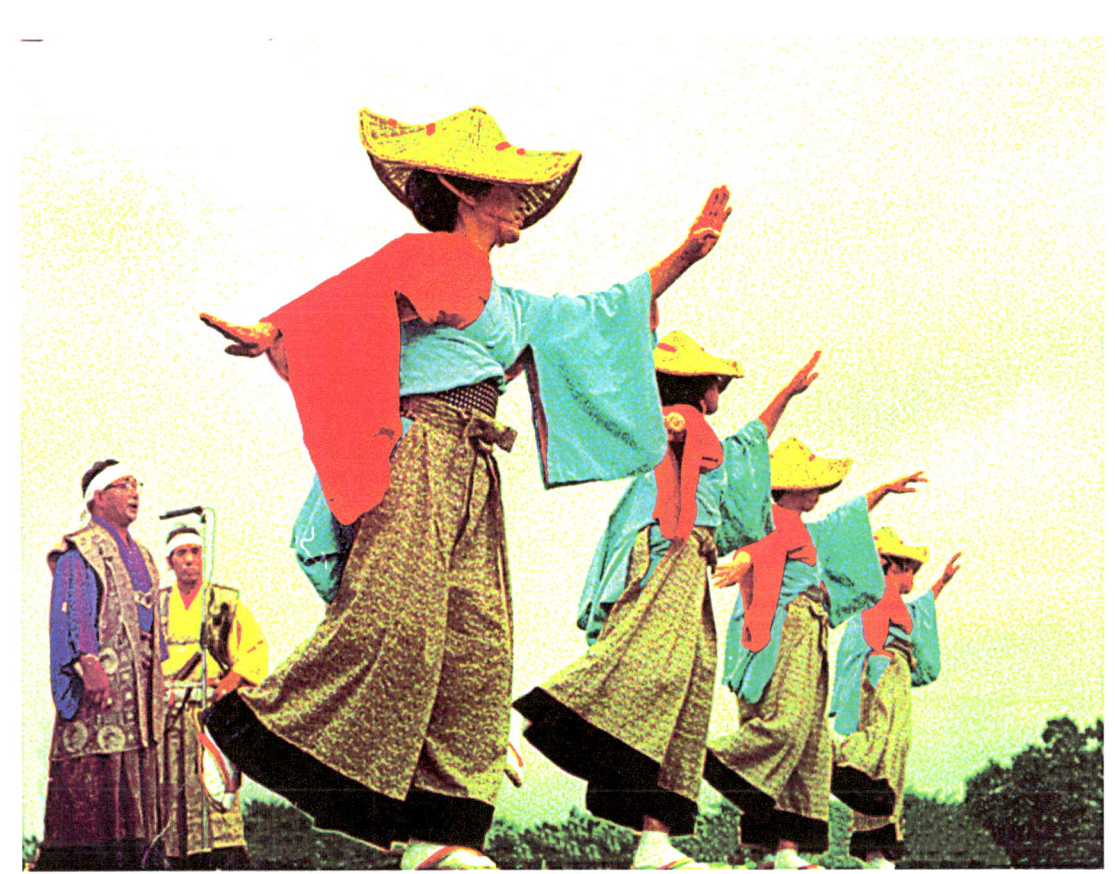

A princess of central India.

Besides the ruins of a Moghul fortress, this beautiful young lady tends a vegetable stall. She looks far older than her thirteen years, yet she wears her threadbare scarf and jewelry with the sophistication of a Hindu princess.

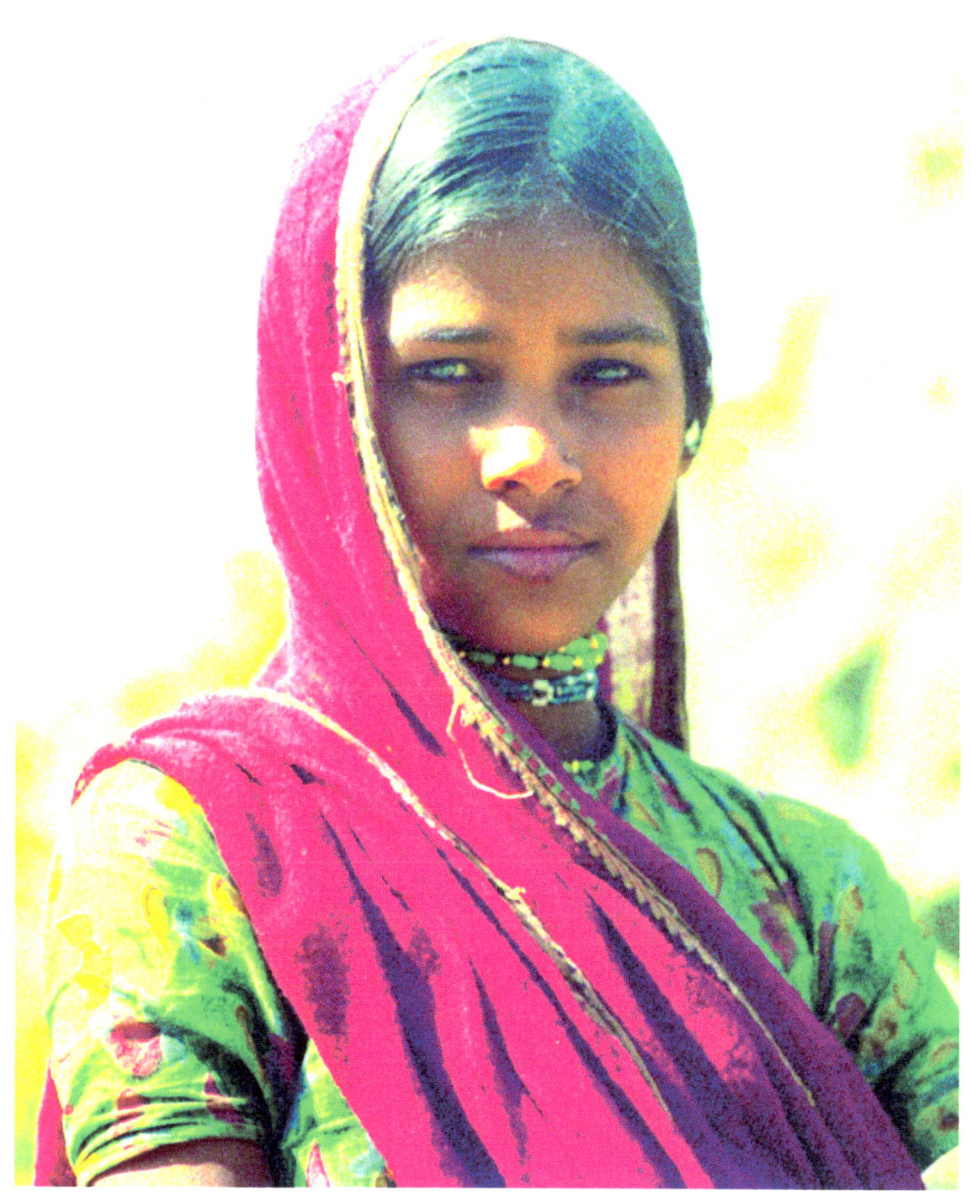

Above the canals of Venice.

A few windows across the canal, seen from
another window.  Yet almost anyone seeing this
simple Mondrian-like composition … even those
who have never been here, know at once, that
this is in Venice, Italy.

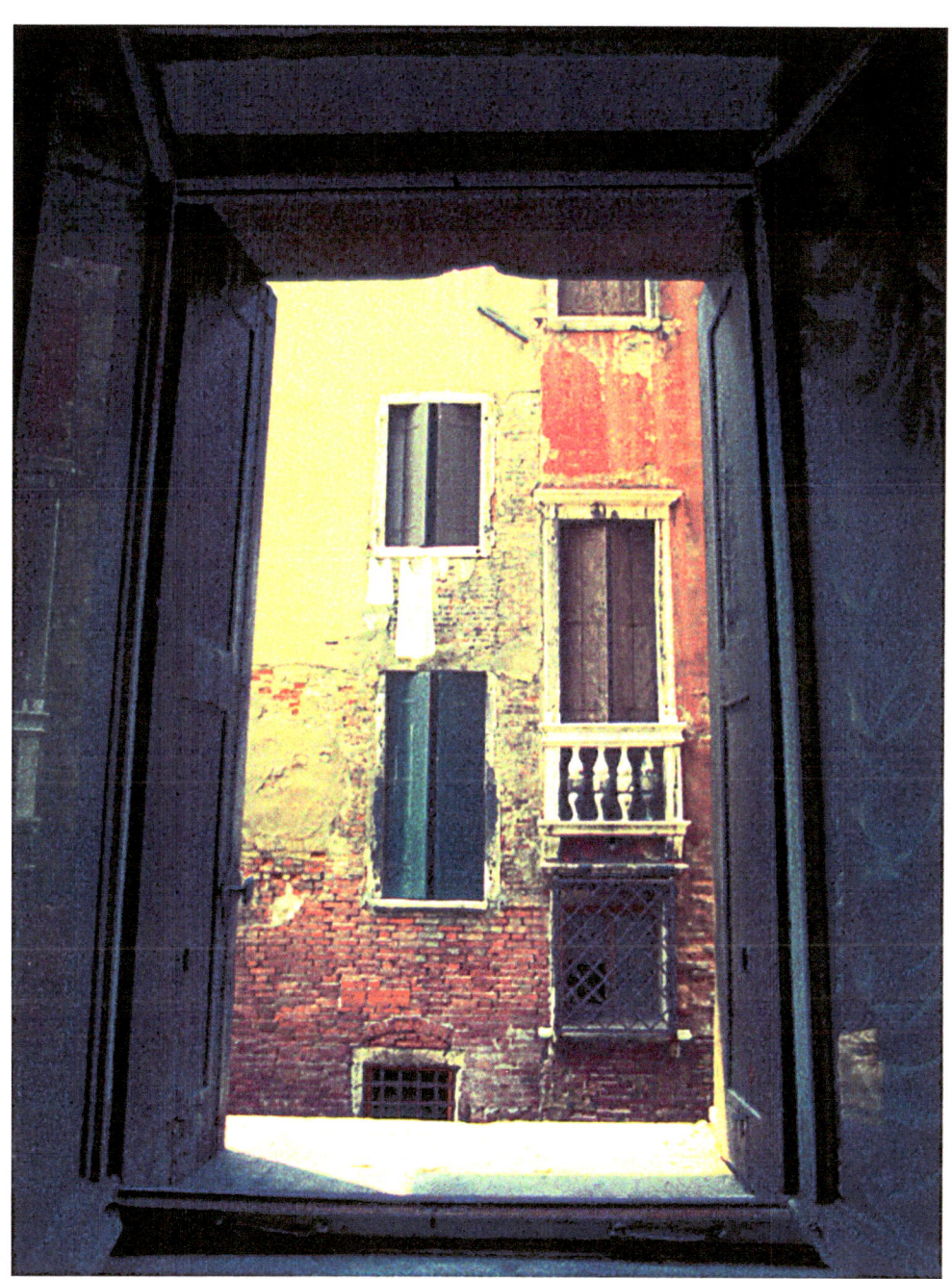

Searching for the past...
(1970)
The Mumzewas, Earl and Vivian, of the Hopi
tribe, Arizona.  In this canyon they examined ...
and read ... petroglyphs, the rock drawings left
by their ancestors, that recorded migration
stories of their clans.
Earl was a priest of Walpi, one of the oldest
continuously inhabited villages in the Americas.
He was involved in the famous Hopi rain
dances, using rattlesnakes in ceremonies to
plead with the Kachina spirits to bring rain to
their fields,  and peace to the world.

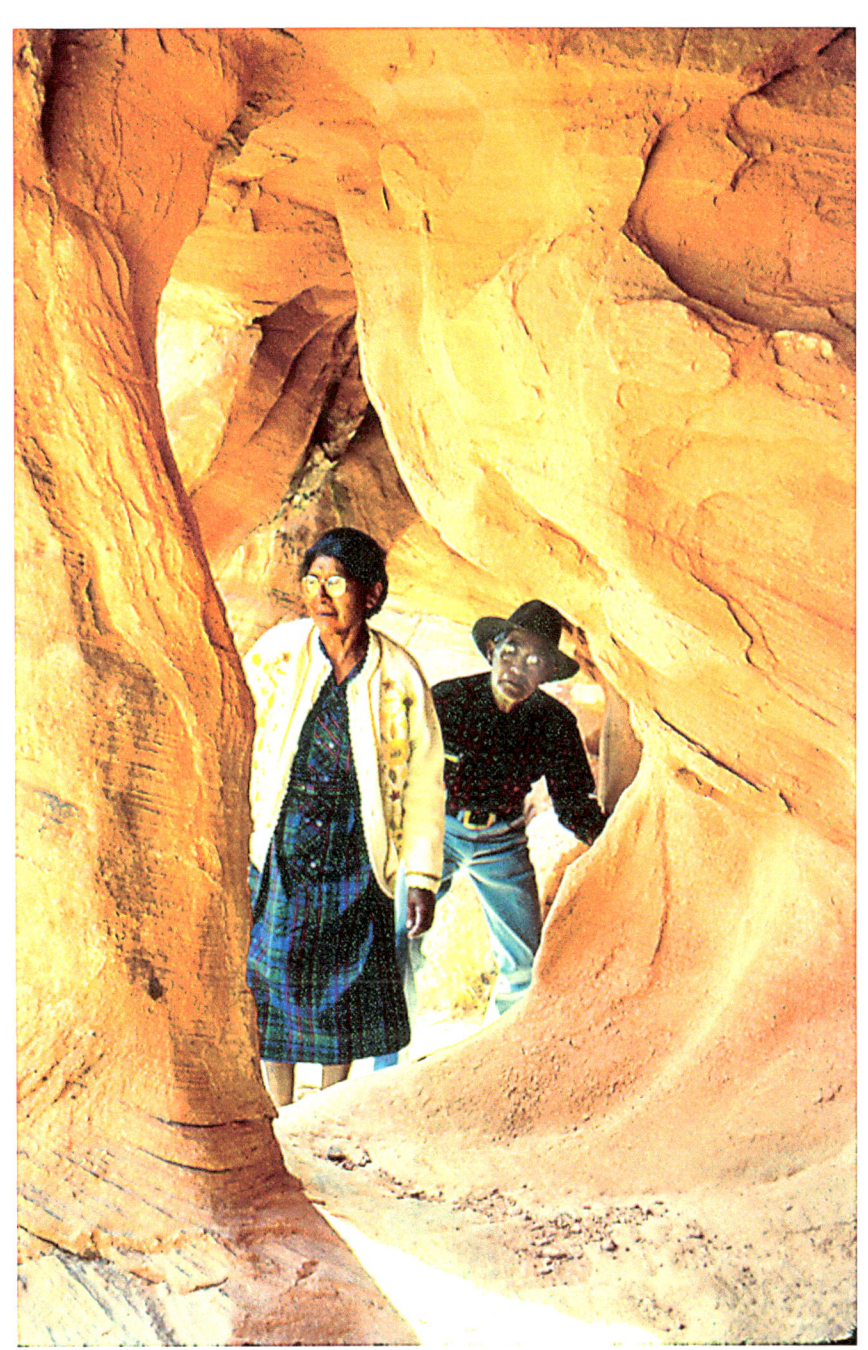

West of the Himalayan Mountains

in the remote fabled valley of Hunza, on the
border of Kashmir and Chinese Turkistan …
a victory dance.
It used to be performed by the warriors after
winning a battle.  Now, this one is only by the
winning team of a polo match … a game which
they swear originated here.  But the drumming,
exotic oboe playing, and flashing of swords is
just as wild today as in the old days.

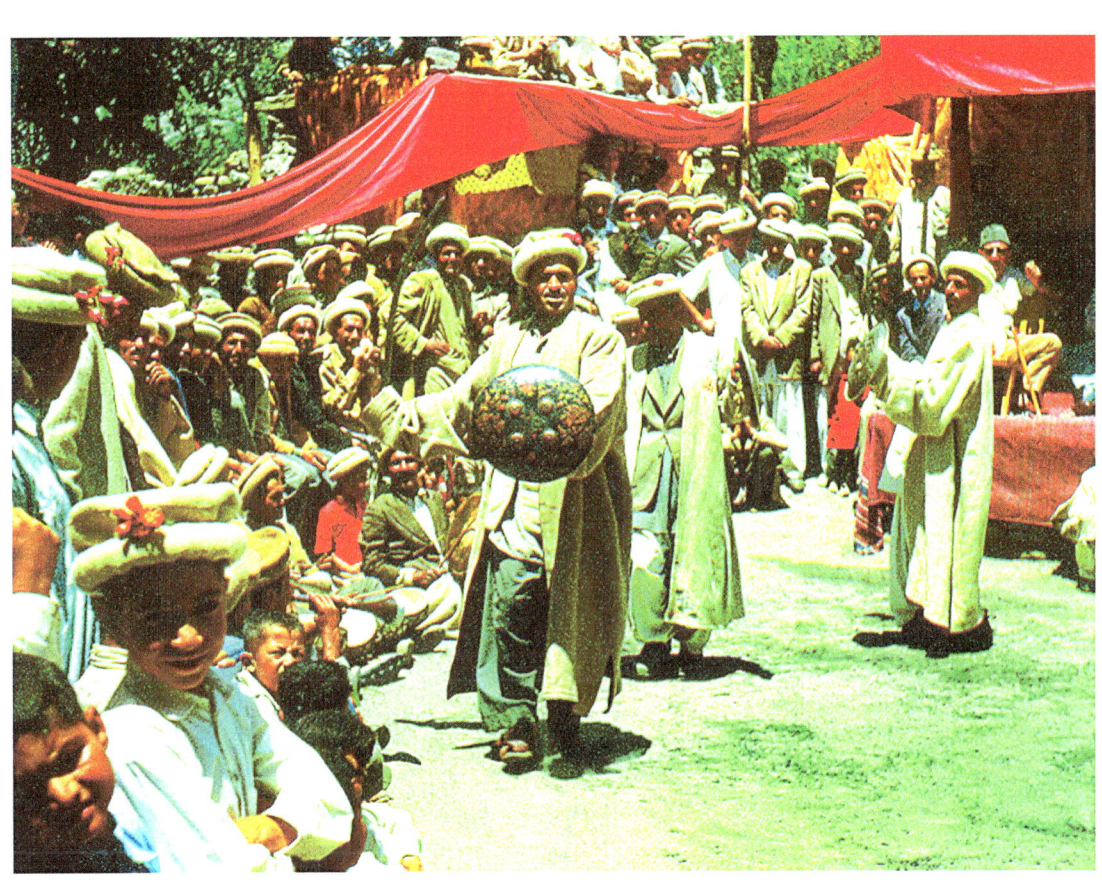

Ceremonial mask of A Northwest Indian dancer,
Vancouver Island, Canada.

Beneath the button blanket, he pulls strings that
open the mask to reveal another mask …
perhaps a death face.

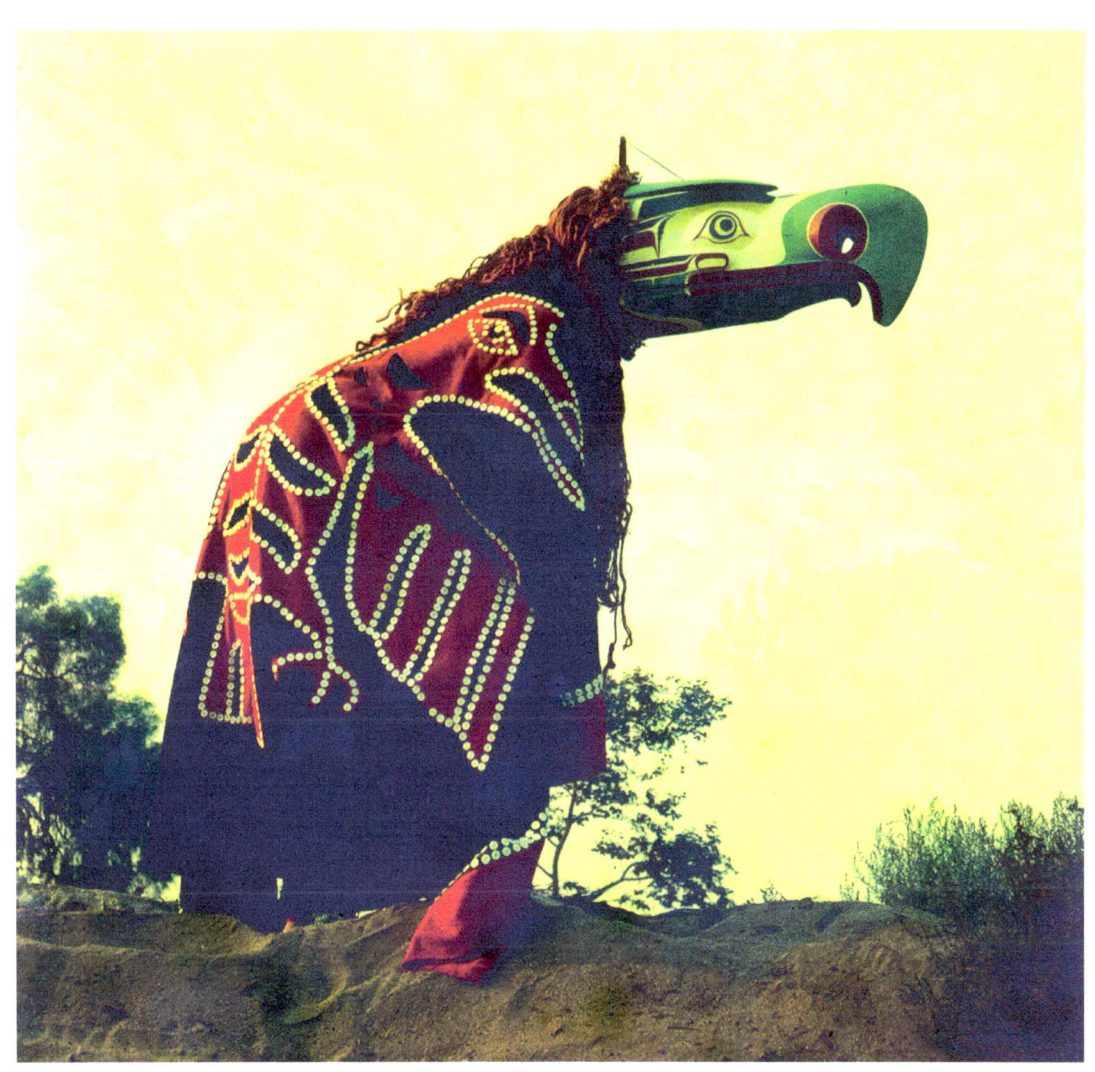

**Classic Thatched British house**

**There still are a few from the old days.  They're not castles, but they probably now cost about the same.**

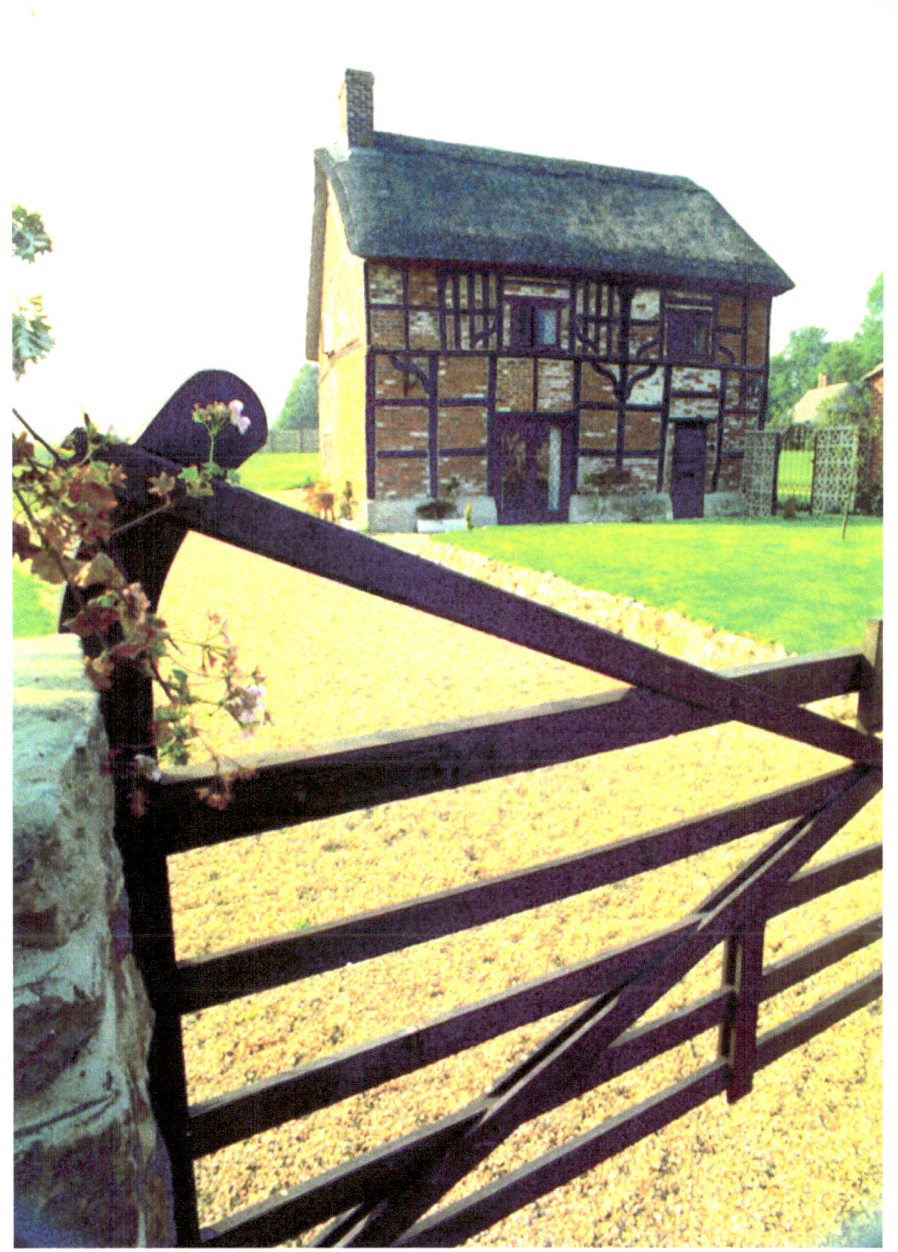

Guatemalan Indian weaving.

Guatemala still has the highest percentage of
Amerindians in any nation of North America,
in spite of the past genocide killings.
This weaver has woven all the clothes that she
and her baby are wearing.  She sells most of her
beautiful creations in a local village market,
receiving only a few pennies an hour for all her
time-consuming work.

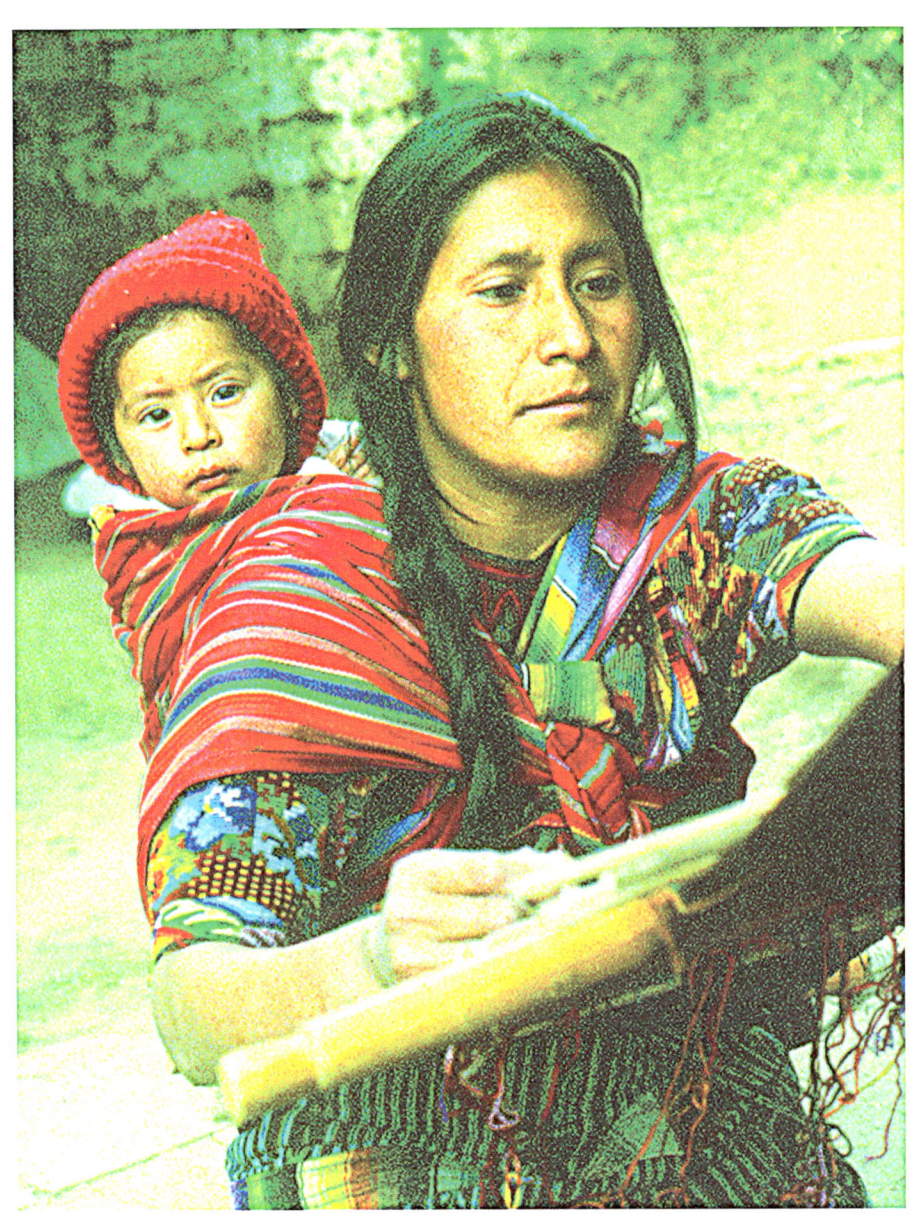

Afghan children weaving.

Nomadic tribes near Muzar-I-Shariff
(remember the terrible fighting there a few years
ago?). They settle down along the Afghan-
Turkistan border to weave their famous
"Oriental Carpets".  Much hand labor is
required, but some carpets can sell for over a
thousand dollars.  They raise their own sheep,
shear the wool, dye it, spin it, and even the
children help in the weaving.
Their small fingers are best for intricate designs.

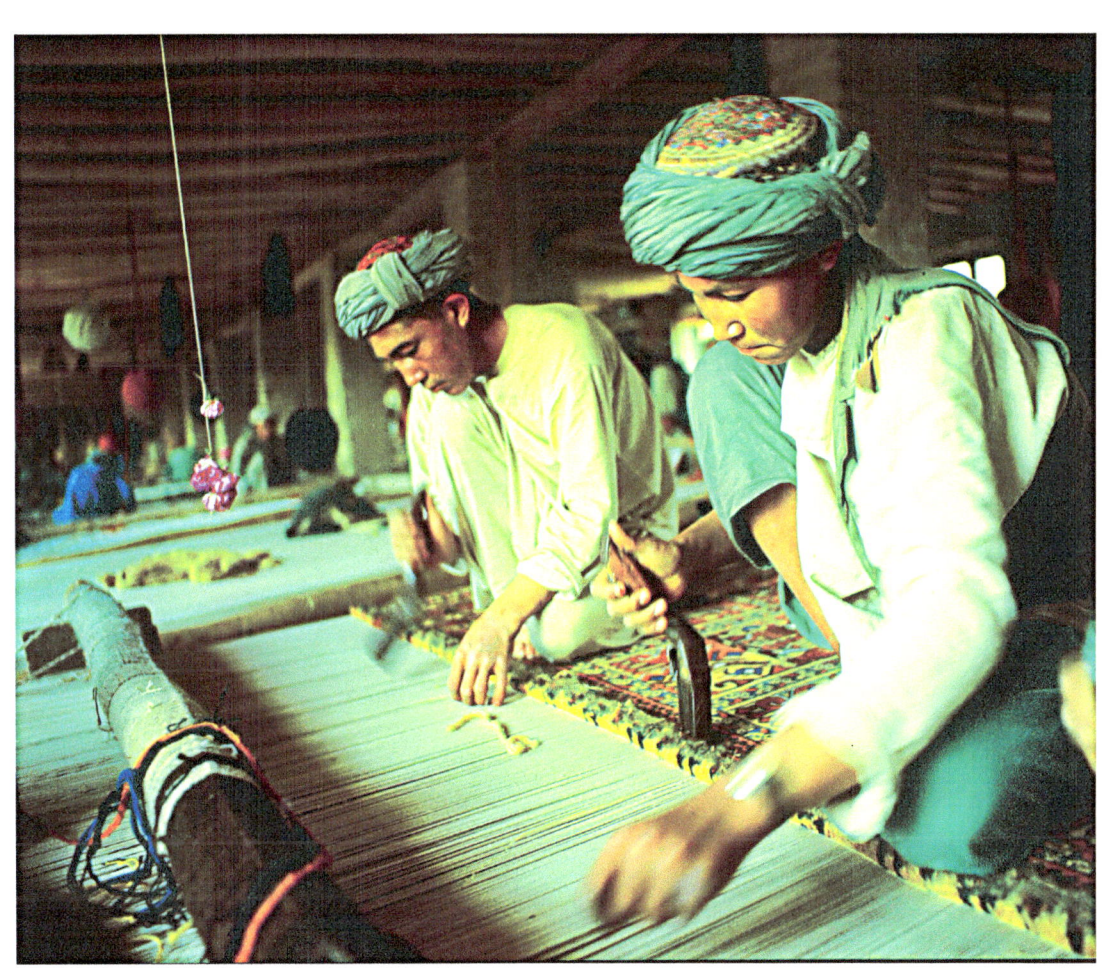

The Atlantic coast of Portugal.

The Portuguese may no longer be the great
explorers of Ferdinand & Esabella's day,  but
their coastal fishing boats have not changed …
designed to rough the Atlantic waves.

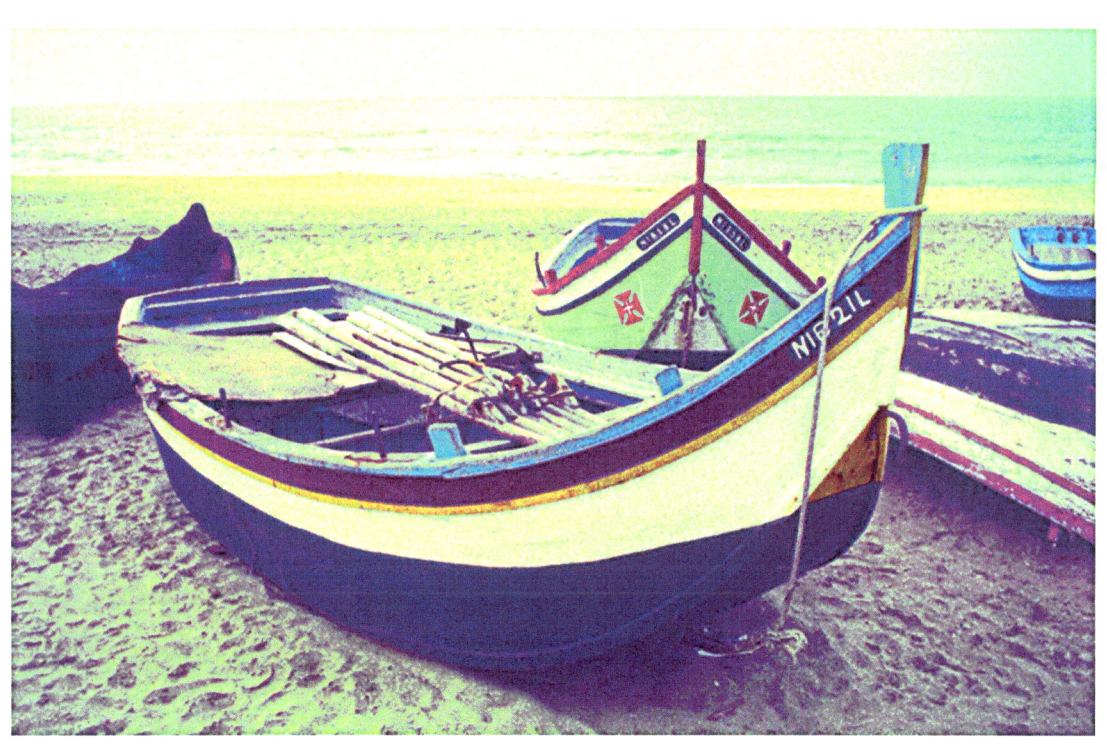

Dawn on the Sulu Sea.

In the mist and calm, along the seas between
Borneo and the Philippines, a family of Bajao
"Sea Gypsies" cast their nets for breakfast.
Their entire lives are lived on this outrigger
houseboat.  They travel  as nomads throughout
the year among the thousands of coconut
covered islands of Southeast Asia.

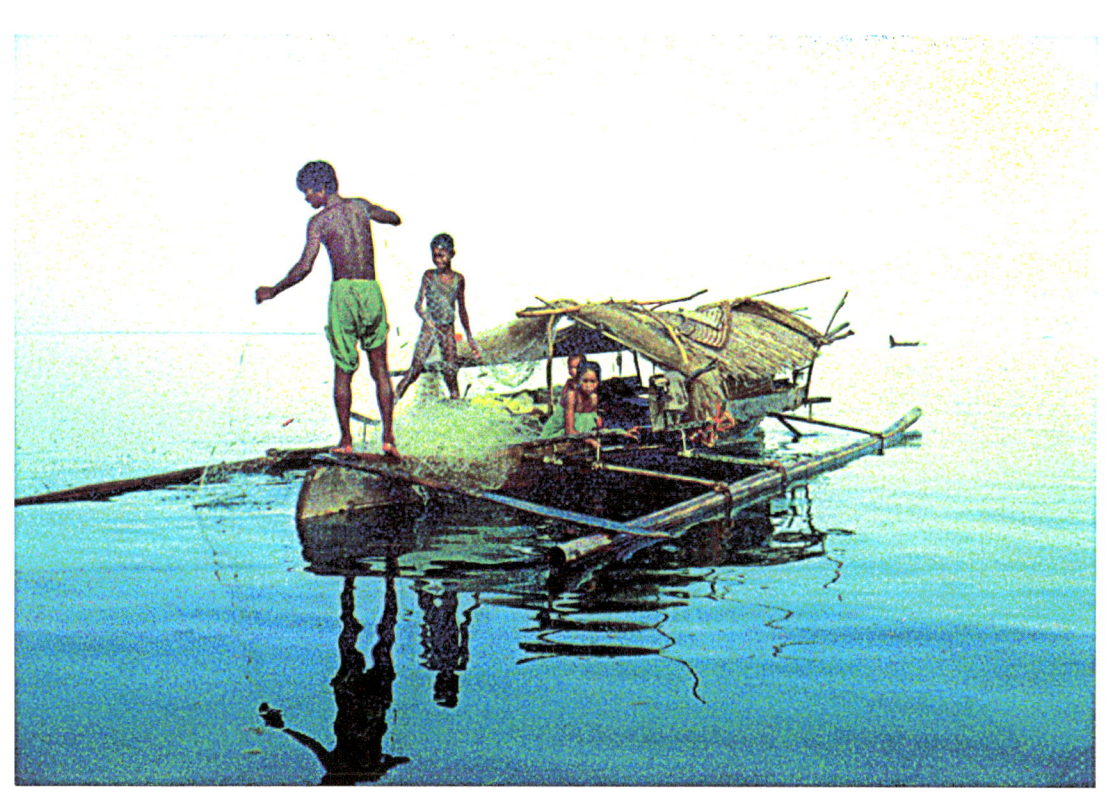

## Whistle Blower

New Guinea tribes dance in their villages for spiritual-
ceremonial reasons. But once every two years or so
they travel through the jungles and hills to the ceremonies
where all the tribes set aside traditional animosities,
and dance for the pure joy of it.  As they enter the huge
dance compound, all metal weapons are taken away.
Only stone axes and spears are allowed in.

Bodies are rubbed in pig fat, and traditional costumes
are worn (plus metal whistles for the dance leaders).
Some tribes have only a dozen dancers, while others may
have more than a thousand.

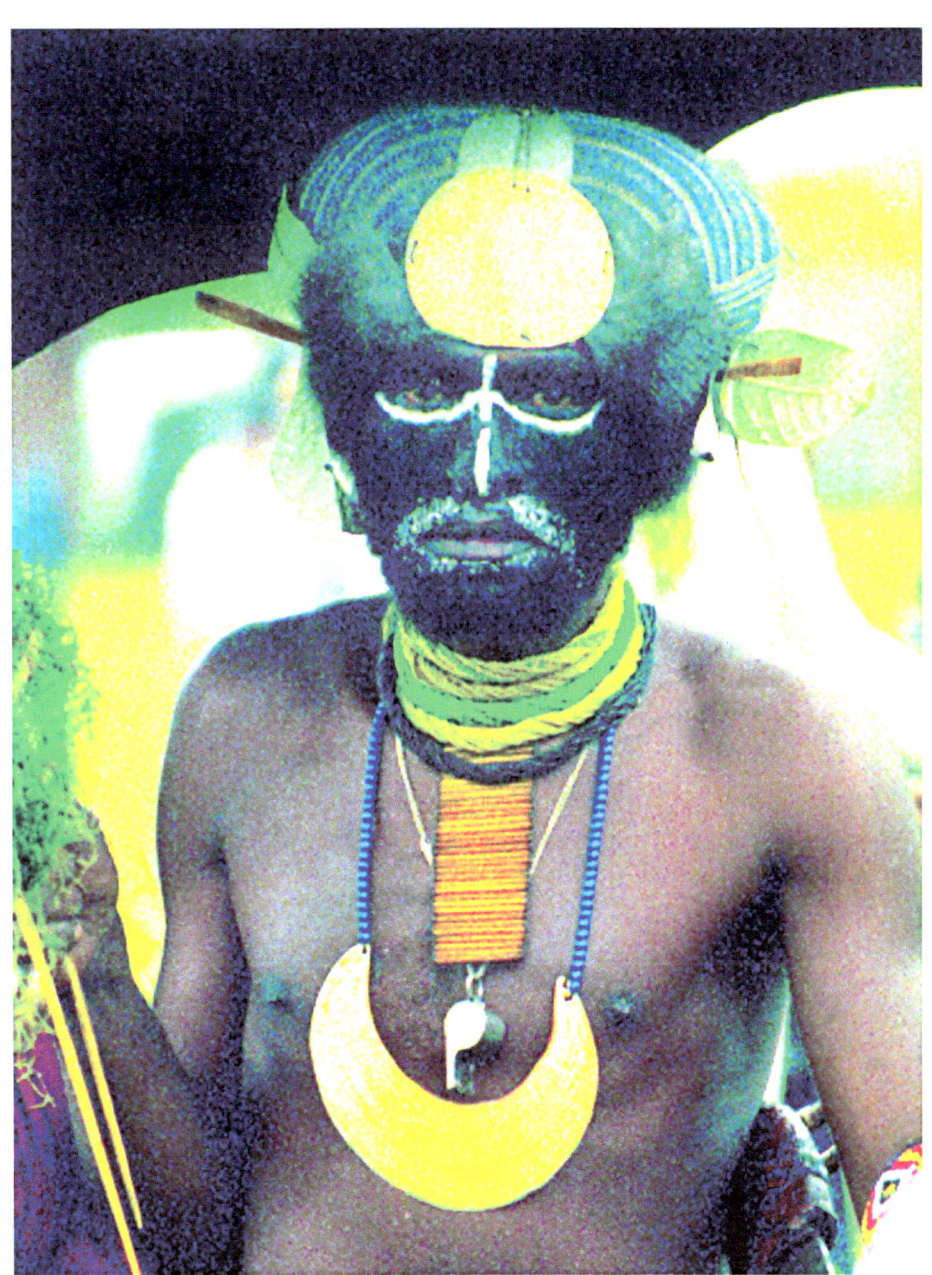

## A Mix of Cultures

In India, the classical Kathak Dance developed from a combination of both Hindu and Mogal traditions. The costume of this famous dancer, Uma Sharma, shows the colorful influence of its Rajastani heritage (Northwest India) where clothing is still the most colorful of all India.

The vibrations of her feet on the bare earth, and the syncopated accompaniment of the Tabla drums and sitar, supposedly matches Lord Shiva's pulsating dancing to bring a sleeping Nature to life.

This 13th century fort, with its famous tower of Quto Minar, on the outskirts of Delhi, is one of the few to have both Hindu and Mogul influences in its architecture and decoration, as does the Kathak dance.

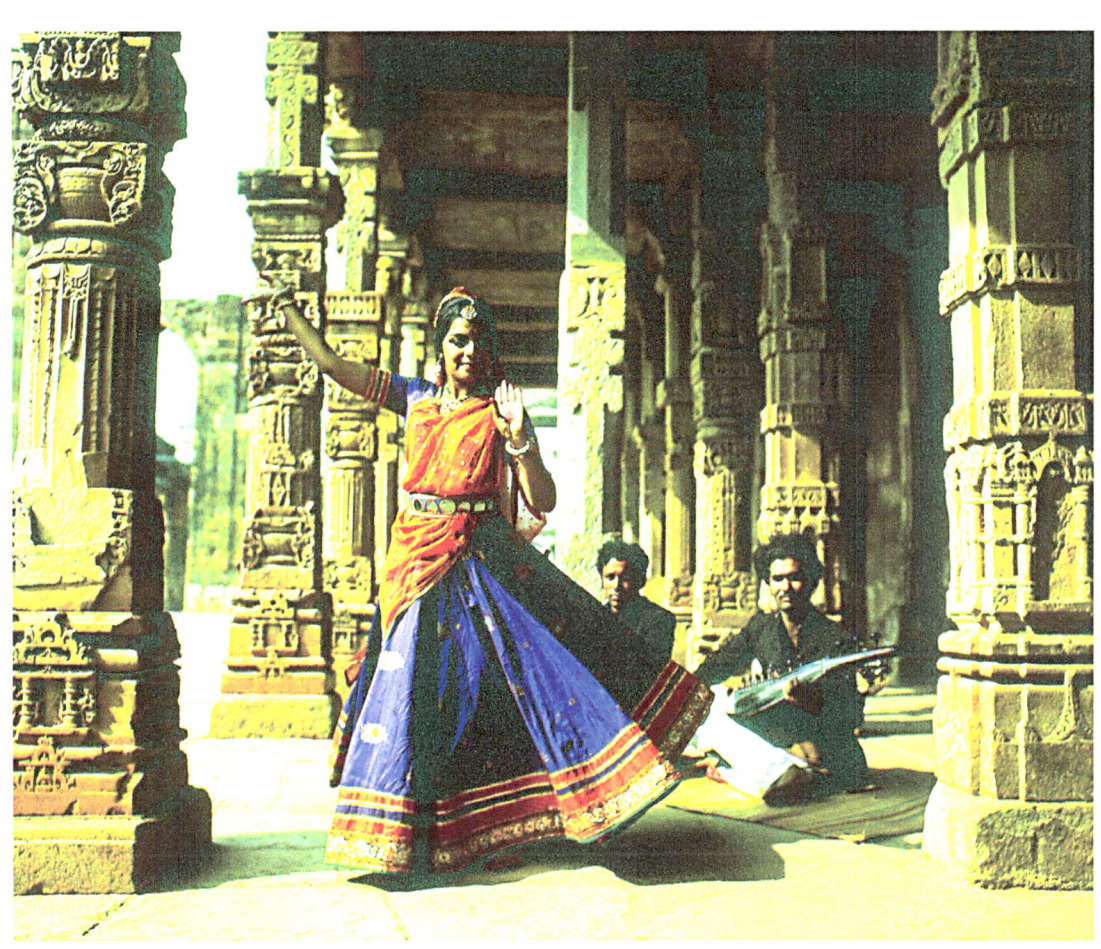

*A Geranium by any other name*
*Could not smell half so sweet.*

Just a single flower on a farmhouse porch
In Romania.
Yet in this simple setting it becomes
a work of art.

50.

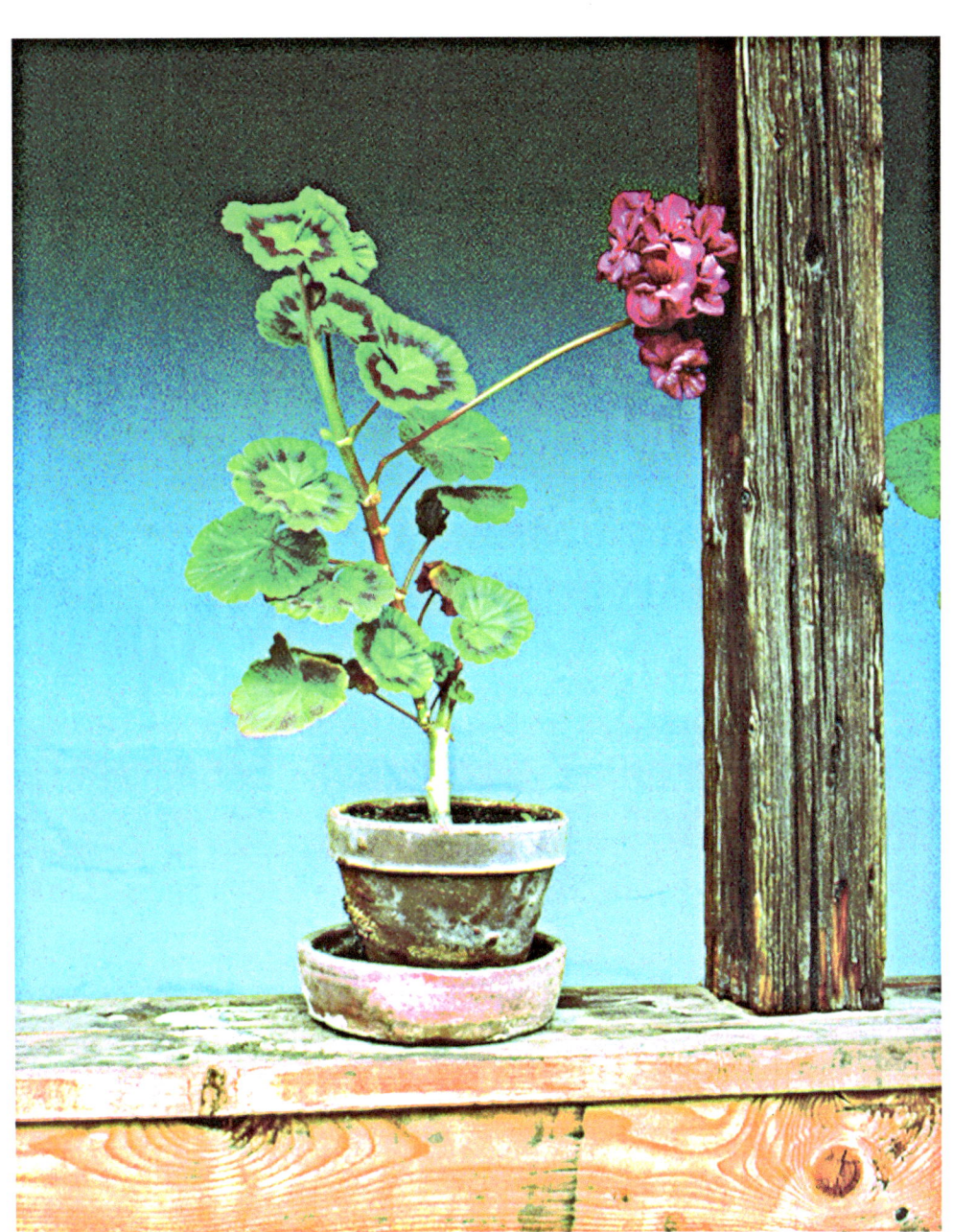

A Touch of Tradition
1956

Vivian Mumzewa, famous Hopi Indian potter, in
her wedding dress, holding an example of her
art.  1st Mesa, Arizona

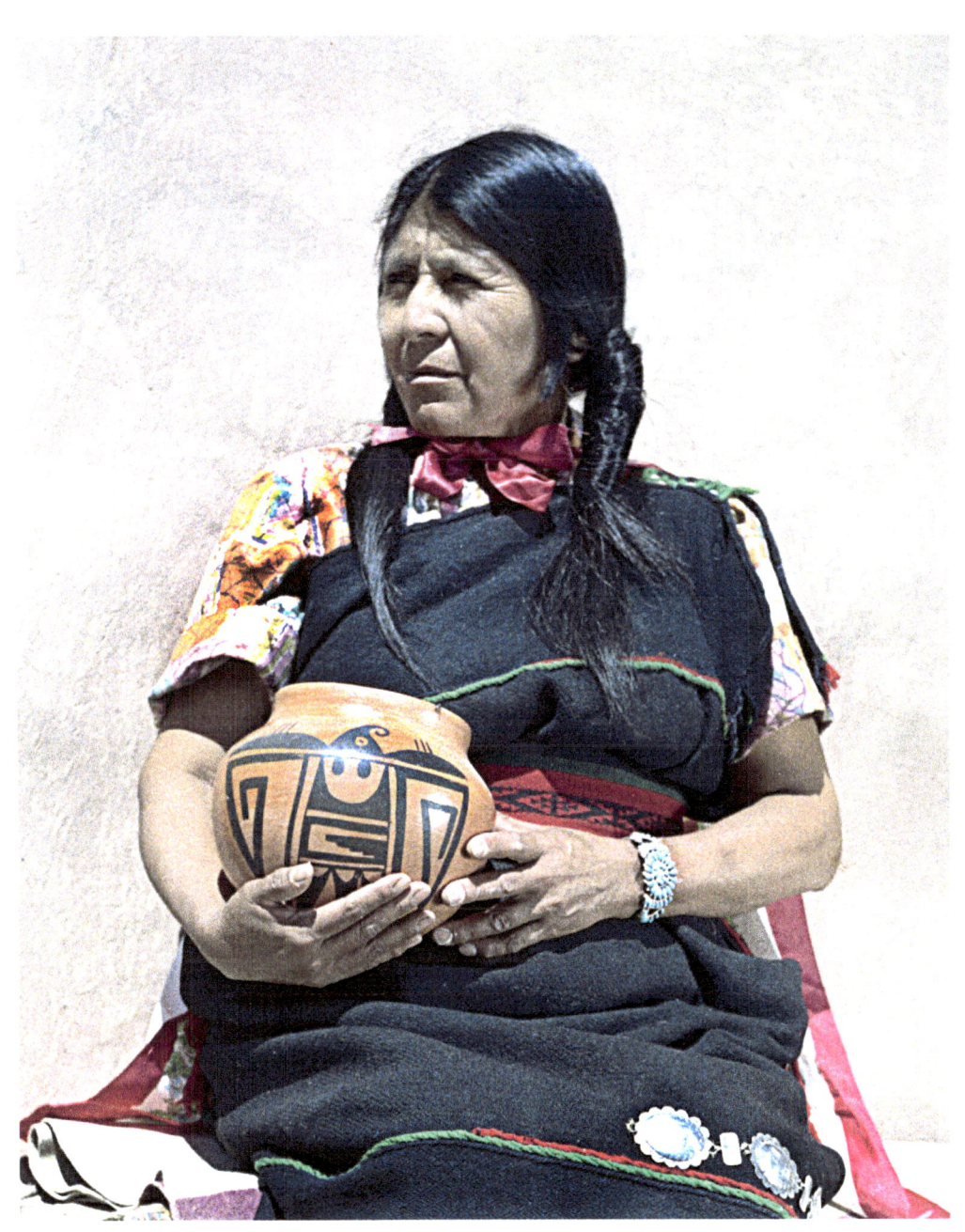

Coconut Gathering on Samoa

To people of tropical islands, coconuts are a
staple, useful in many ways besides food.
As important to them as the buffalo was to the
Plains Indians.

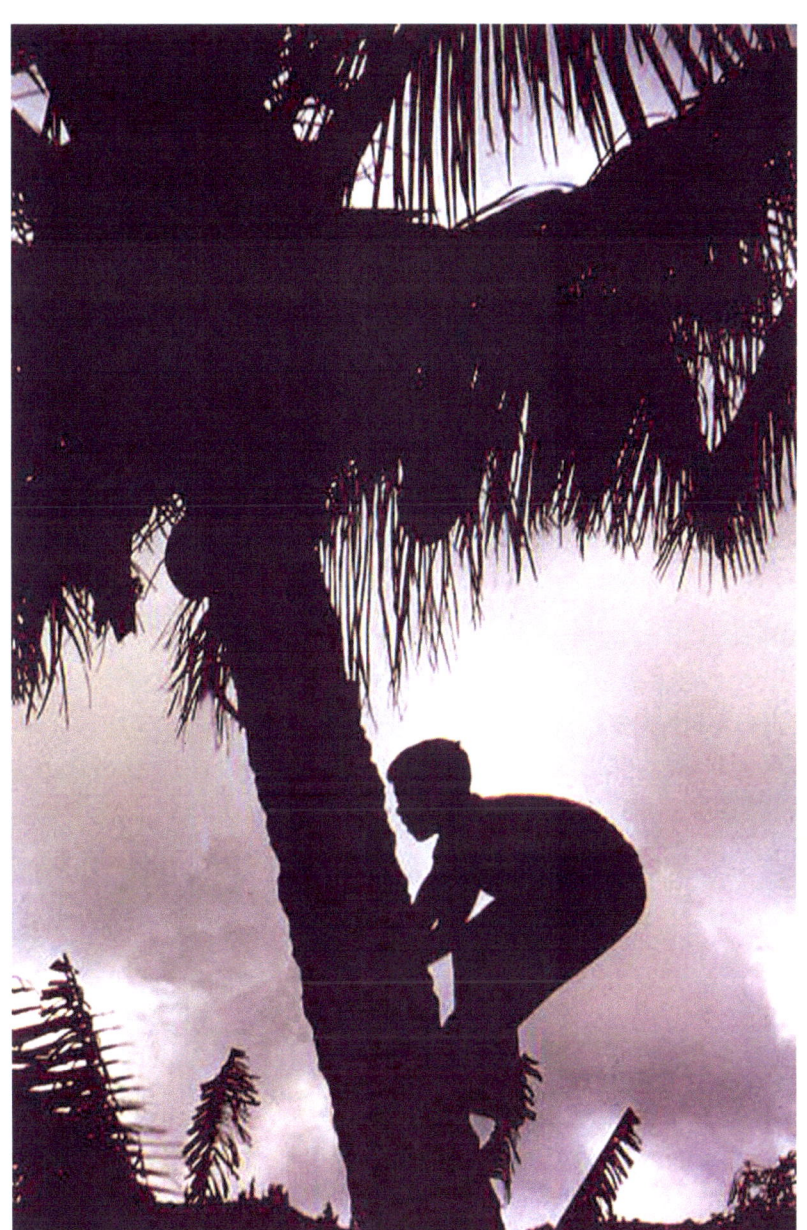

Within a Hindu temple

From the inside of this temple in south India, we see these Trident staffs, which are often carried by wandering Hindu ascetics ... men who have severed all ties with their families, society, and materialism, in their search for personal truths: practicing non-injury of all living creatures, and hoping for release from the cycle of reincarnation.

The priests in this temple insisted that they perform their marriage rites for my companion and me, even though we had been married long ago in a Japanese Shinto Shrine.

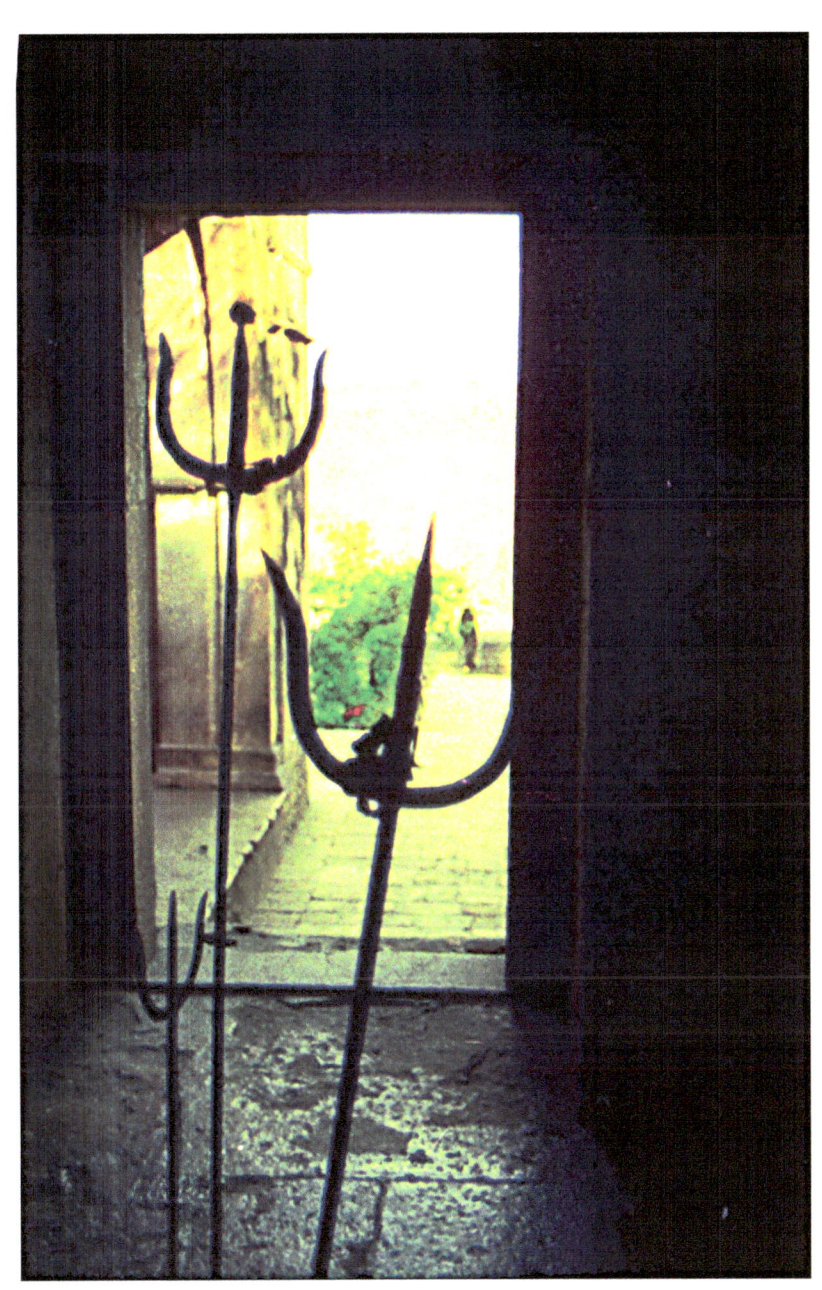

## Dancing in Romania

**The entire village joins in a wedding party … out on the dirt streets in the center of town (no cars there anyhow).**

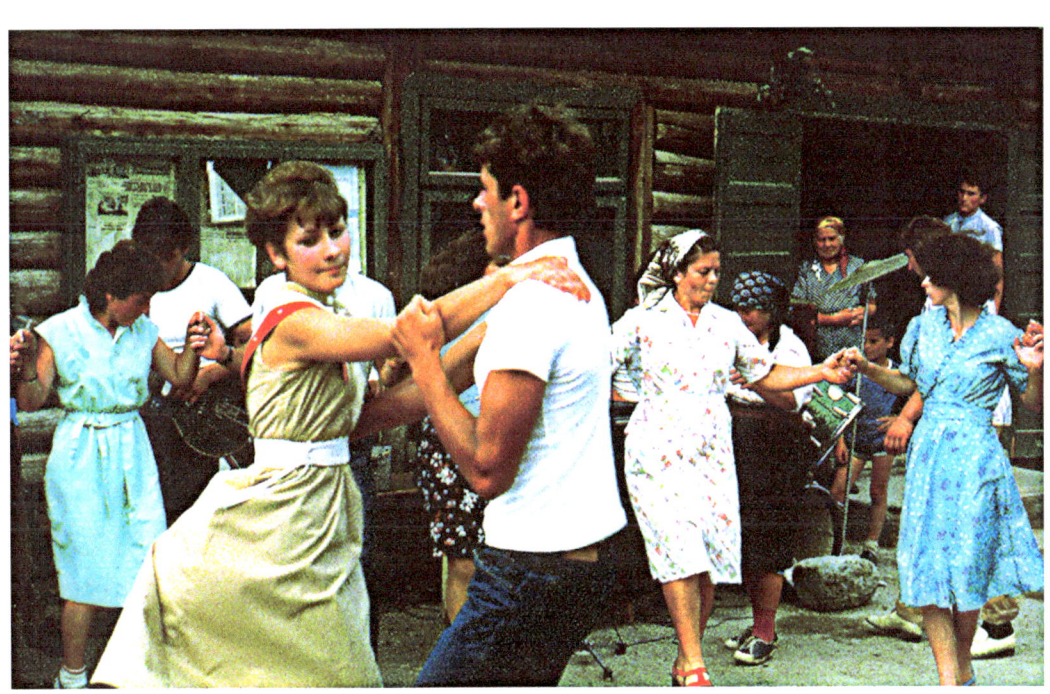

**Wedding party in Nepal**

**Coming down a Himalayan trail, this party
stopped long enough for their musicians to
serenade us … before continuing on, carrying
the young bride (crying) to her new village.**

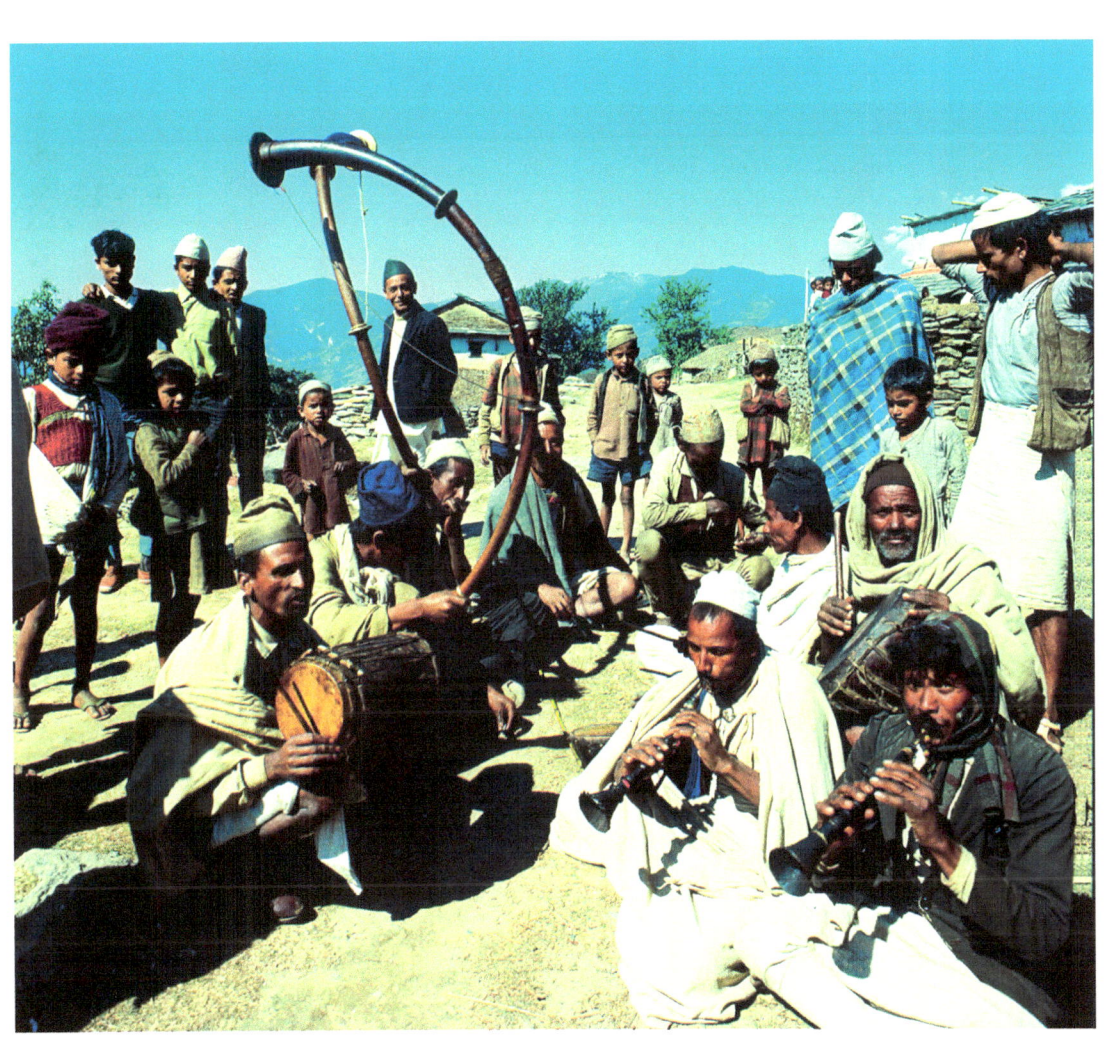

This Scarecrow who had a big smile
was always dressed up in great style.

But when the rains came
he felt terrible shame
'cause his straw ended up in a pile.

This slap-happy fellow can sing.
But scaring crows is not quite his thing,

'Cause when he belts out a tune
(sounding like a buffoon)

All the crows gather 'round in a ring.

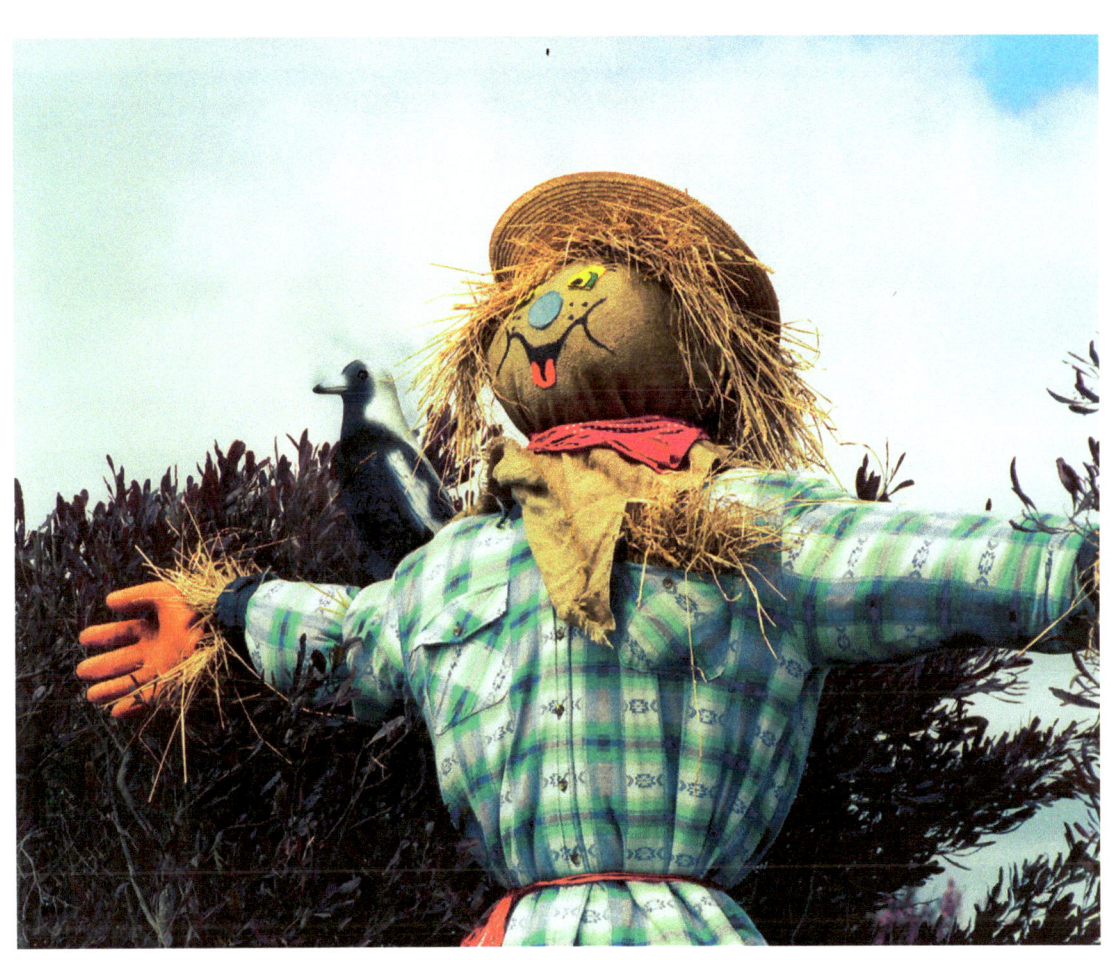

Left by the invaders

An abandoned Mogul fort in the hills of central
India.  Islamic architects were masters of
combining arches for strength and for beauty.
As they conquered across Asia, they brought
their skills producing such masterpieces as the
Taj Mahal, and this great fort … now in ruins and
isolated.

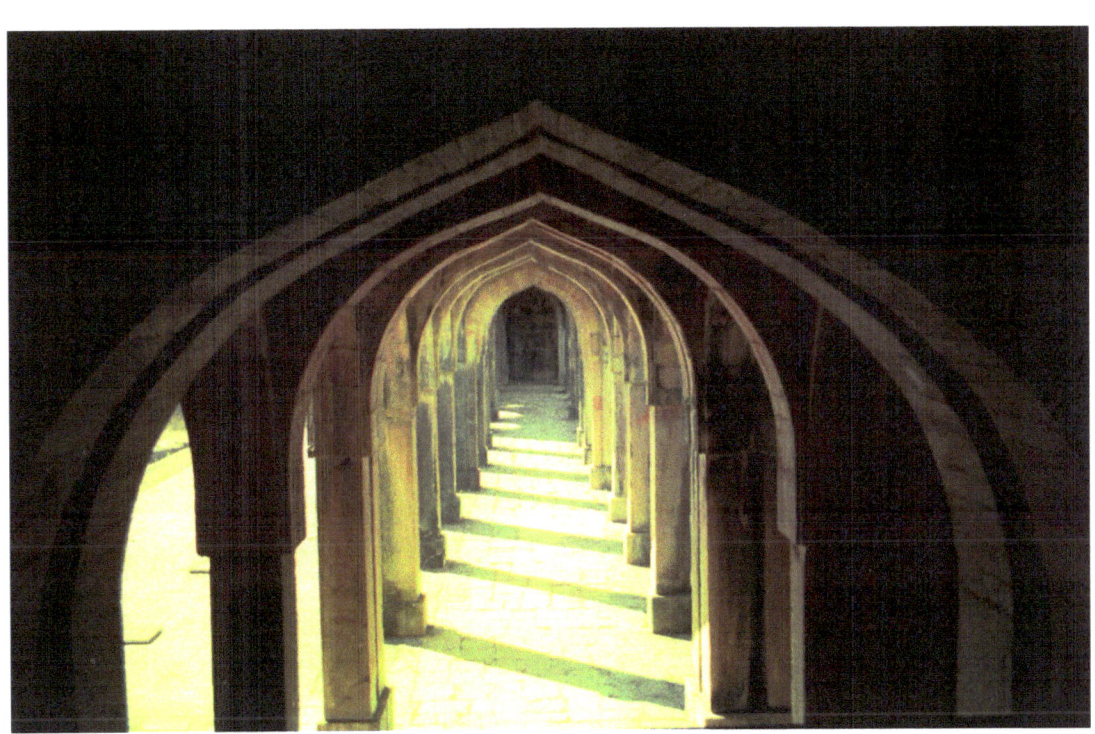

## Mountain Tribes of Thailand

Throughout Southeast Asia, each nation may seem different from each other, at least in some ways. But all their hill tribes are very similar. As we hiked along a narrow jungle trail near the Thai–Burma border, we came upon a clearing with a small village. Everyone greeted us with friendly surprise. These children divided their curiosity between my cameras and our two year old son being carried on my wife's back.

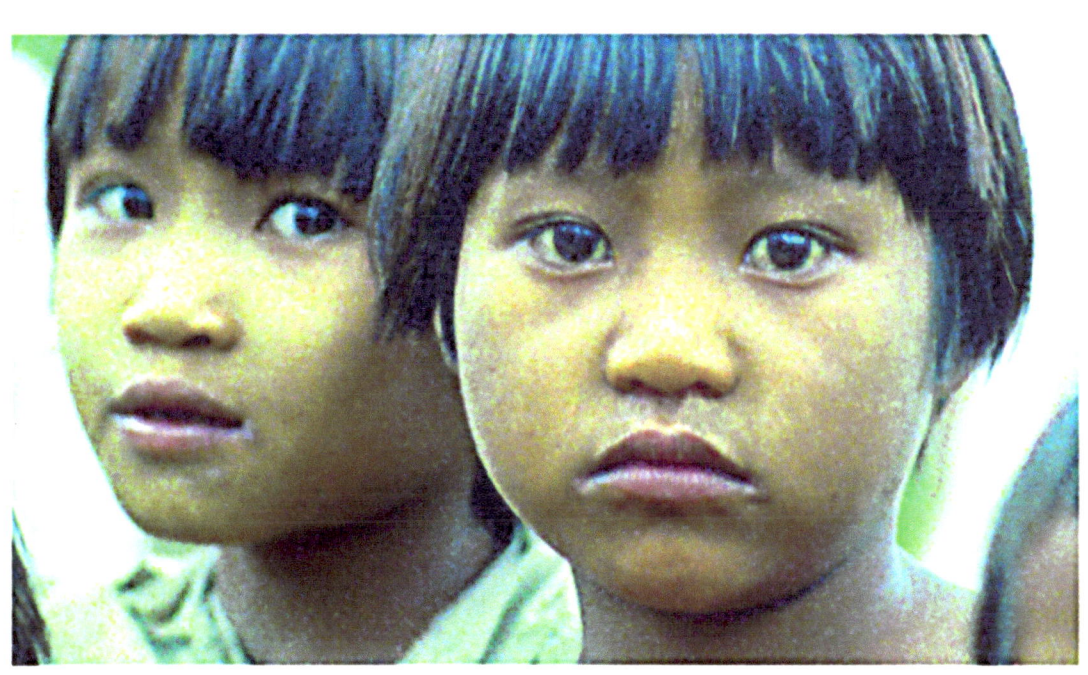

**Bamboo Forest in Autumn**

**The texture, pattern's, and subtle green shades
of bamboo, contrast with the orange maple
leaves carpeting a hillside in Kyoto, Japan.
The calligraphy reads
*"Serenity"*.**

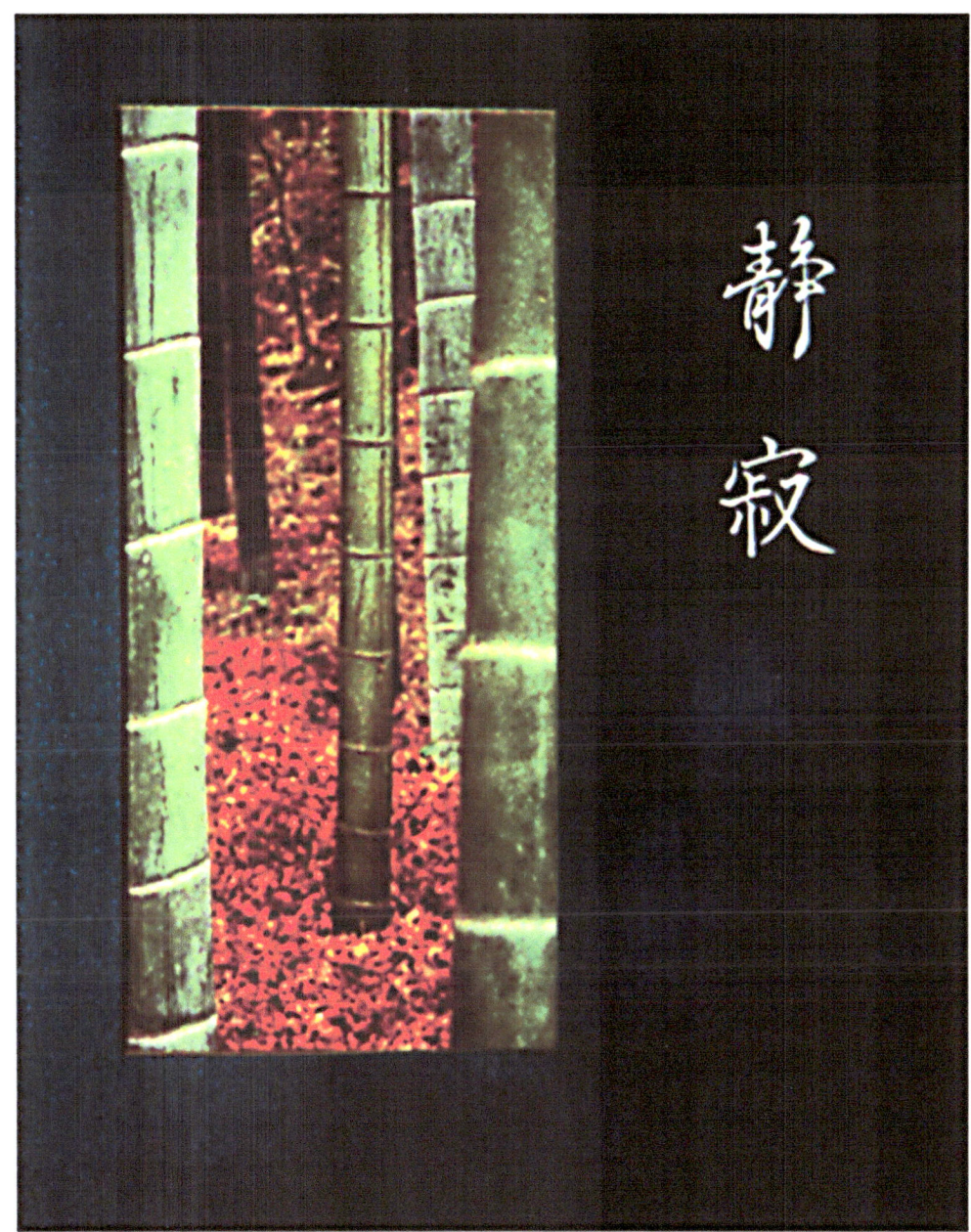

静

寂

## Zen Bamboo

Again, the calligraphy here reads *"Serenity"*.
From the same slide as previous page, yet it has
a different mood.  Quieter, far less realistic.
Viewers seem equally divided in their
preferences between the two compositions.
Except for a neighbor in Japan who asked
"why do you bother wasting film on such
meaningless photos?"
Yet another photographer who was present
when I was trimming the enlarged prints to
produce these compositions, picked up the
trims, joined several together, and produced
another entirely different composition, as good
as … or perhaps better than these.

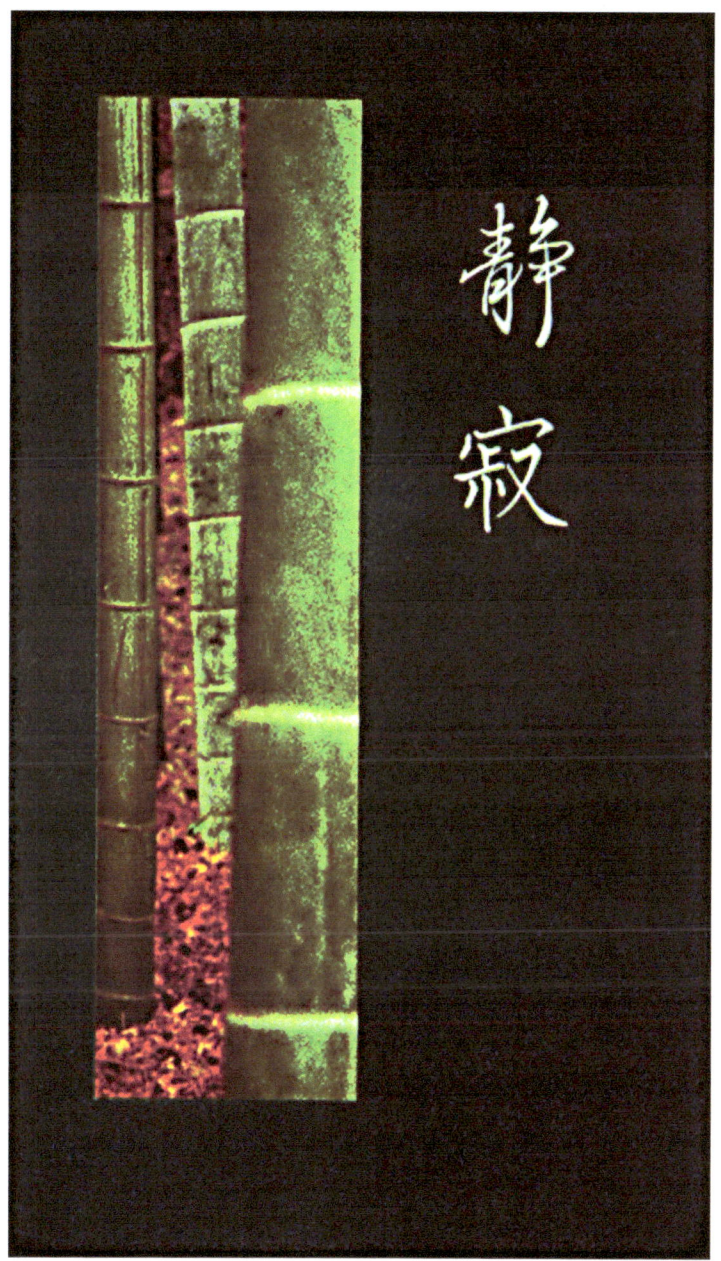

## An Afghan Cover-up

Chador veil and child, at the great mosque of
Harat, western Afghanistan.
The glazed tiles show a favorite theme:
symbolic vase and flowers ... Islamic art cannot
depict life.  With the veil totally covering the
person, we can't even guess who she is, or what
she's like.
And she's been taught to prefer it that way.

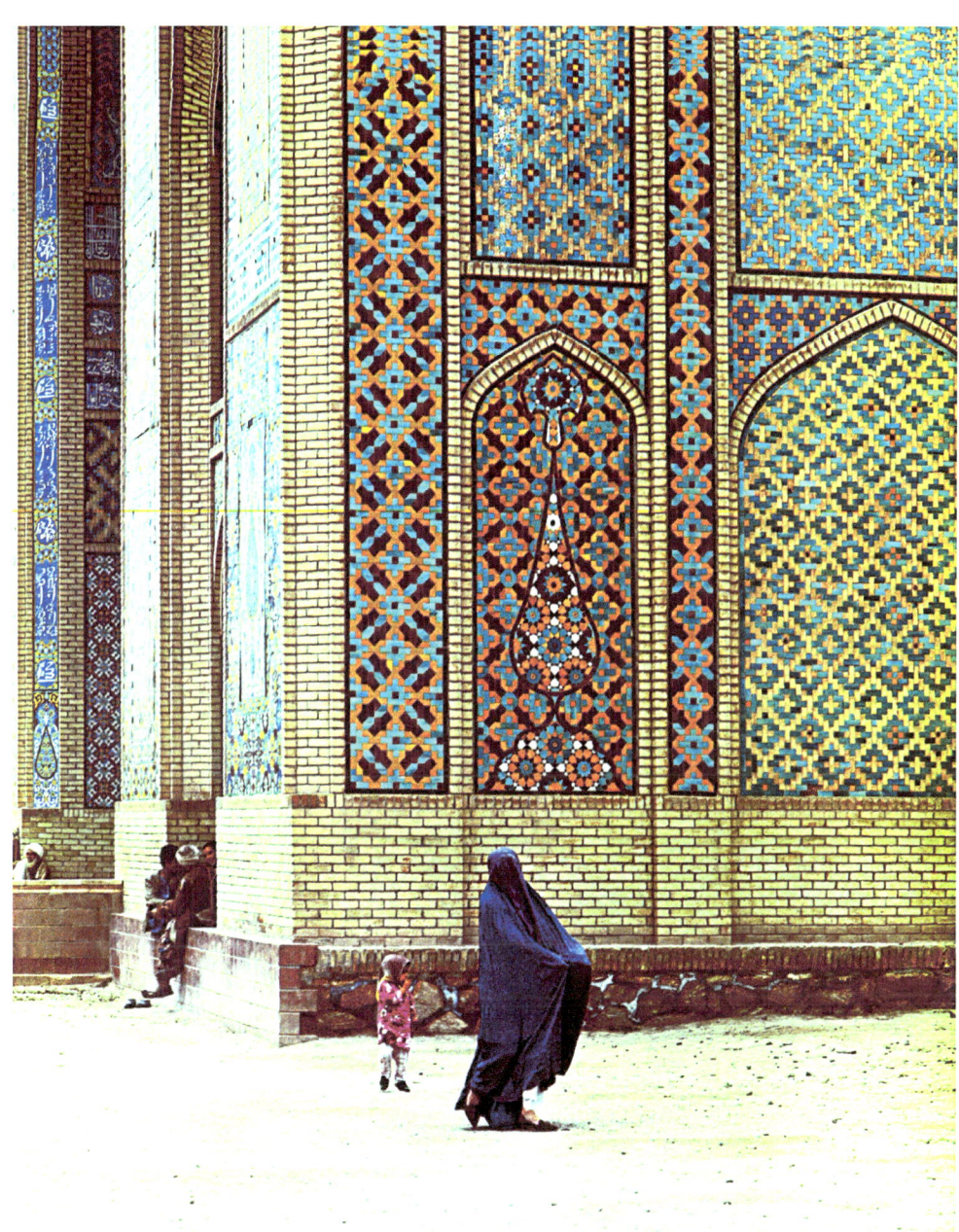

**Glaze Tiled Buddhist Temple Roof**

Practical, strong. They last for centuries.
But combined with architectural artistry, they
become works of Japanese art  that can be
appreciated by people of any culture.

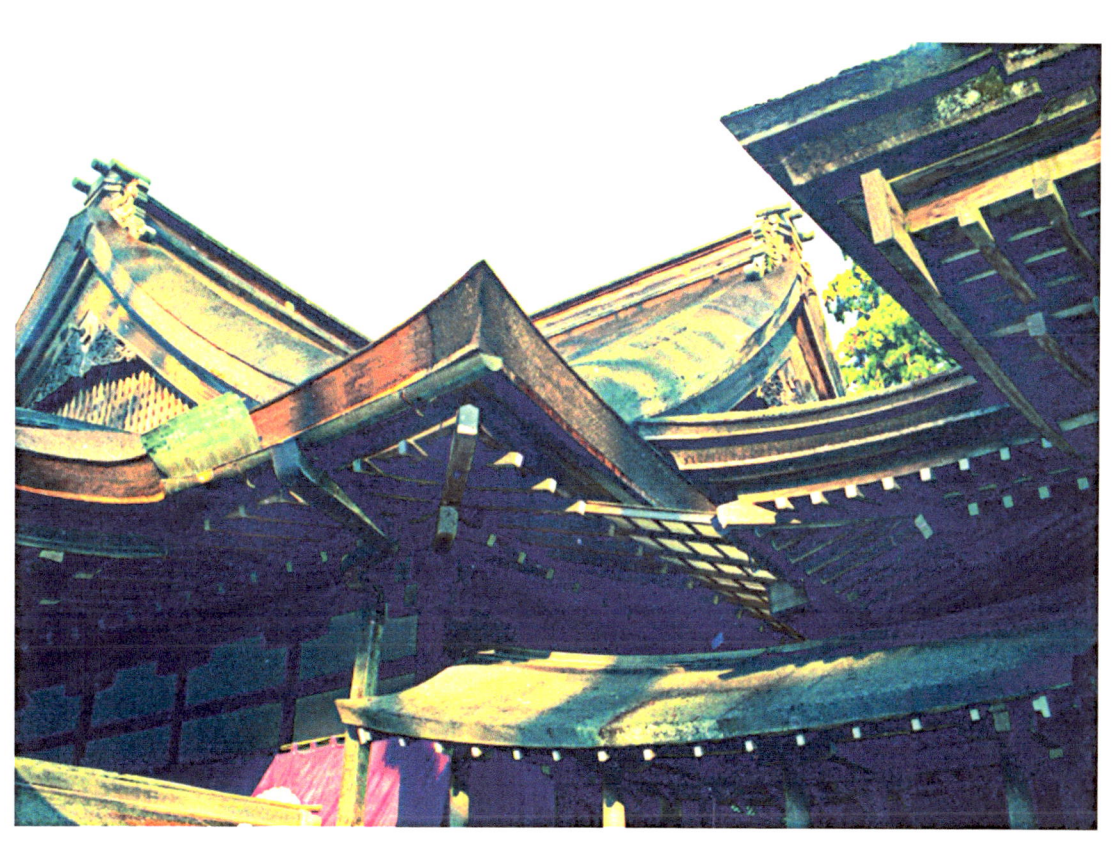

Snowed-In Farm Village

Dawn in the mountains of Japan.

In city apartments rooms are usually
small, but these farm houses have
living rooms large enough for the family
and space to store their crops.
There's even a room for their milk cow.
In the high ceilings, vegetables and
clothing are hung to dry.
Children cannot get out to school, so
they have to board in schools down the
mountain.

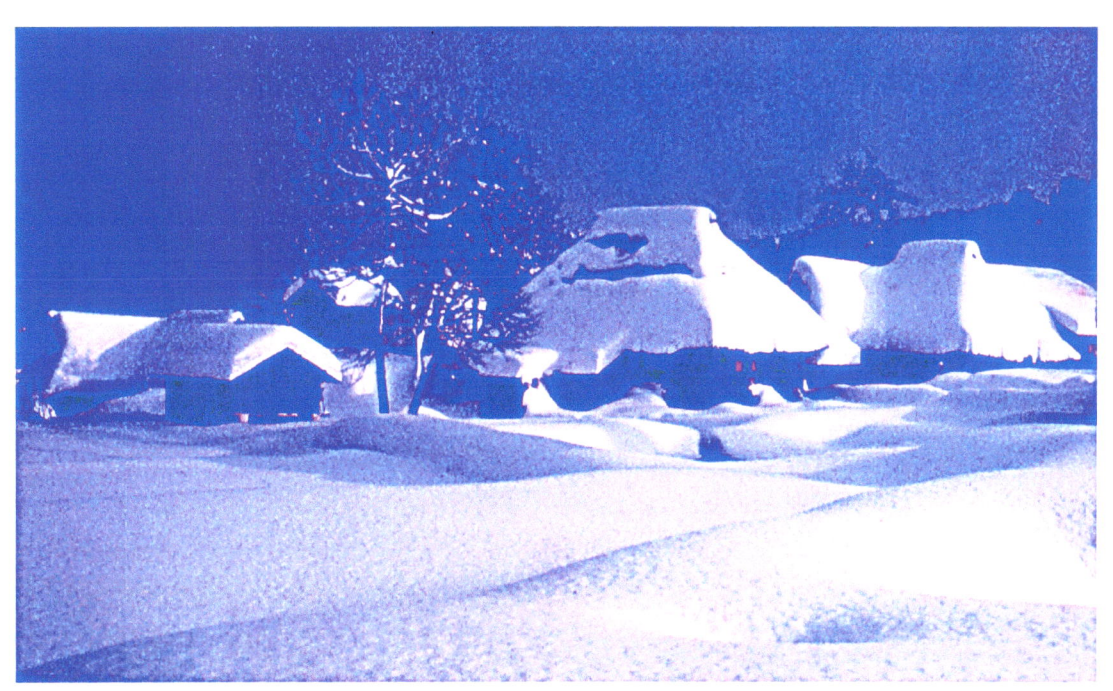

## Temple Boys Entering Festival Grounds

At the annual Samurai Horse Festival near Soma, Japan, these schoolboys in feudal costume are the advance flag-bearers for a Shinto priest who is to bless the festival. August in Japan is hot and humid. yet it is festival month throughout the country. Perhaps to forget the heat, but certainly a time to remind the people of, and give them pride in, their ancient heritage.

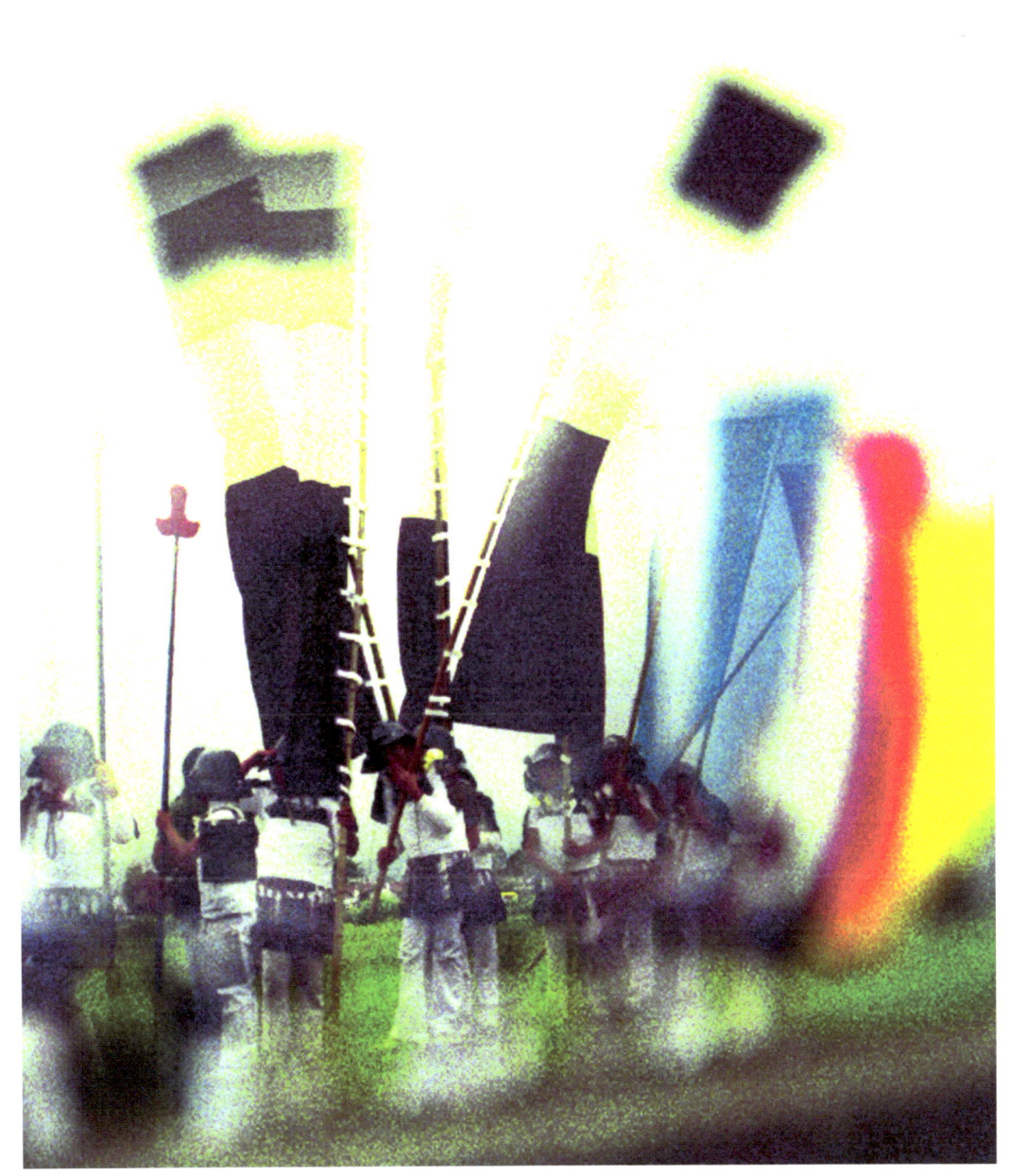

**Hi-Tech in Afghanistan**

Not exactly shooting digital, this photographer
in the ancient grand bazaar of Mazar-I-Sharif,
near the Afghan-Russian border, has his camera
and processing lab all in one box.
"Photos While You Wait"
Just a few decades ago such cameras were
common throughout the U.S. and can still be
seen in much of the third world.

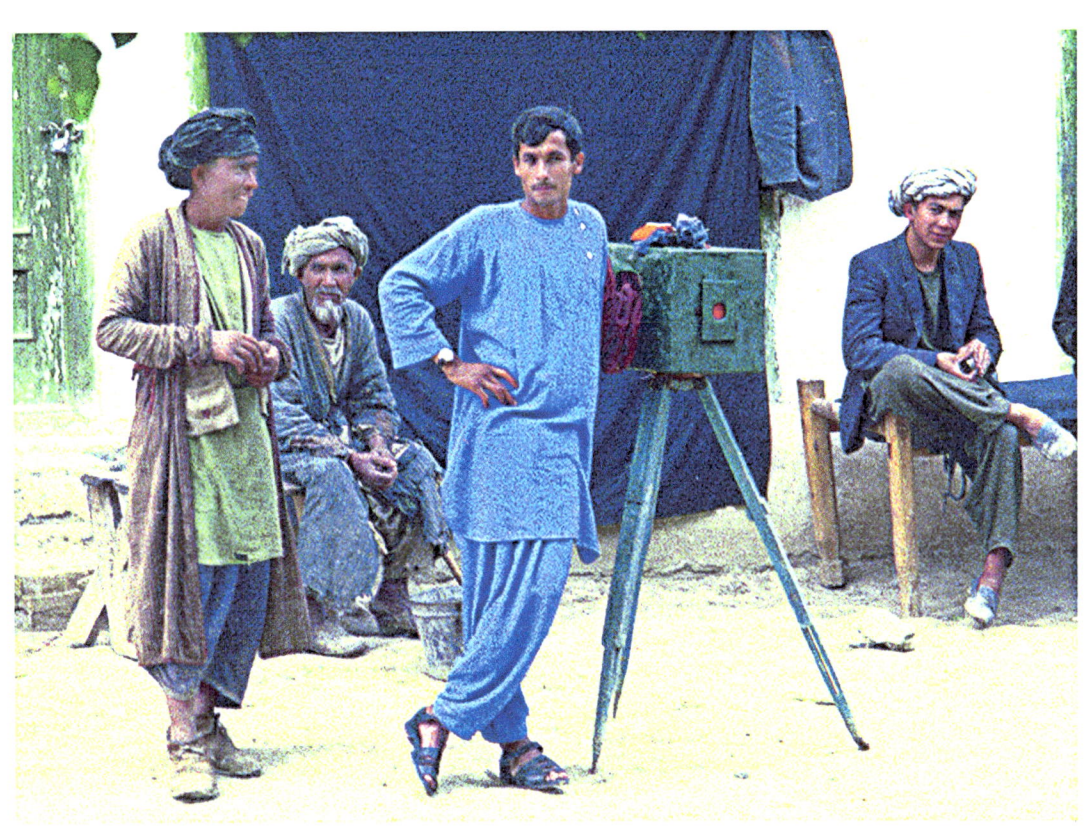

## Shrine Ceremony, Japan

"Vestal Virgins" … Shrine maidens, taking part in a renewal ceremony at the Kasuga Shinto Shrine in Nara, Japan.  First built in 768 CE for the powerful Fujiwara family, it is totally dismantled every twenty years, and rebuilt in a grand ceremony that attracts thousands of devoted Japanese, and tourists from around the world.

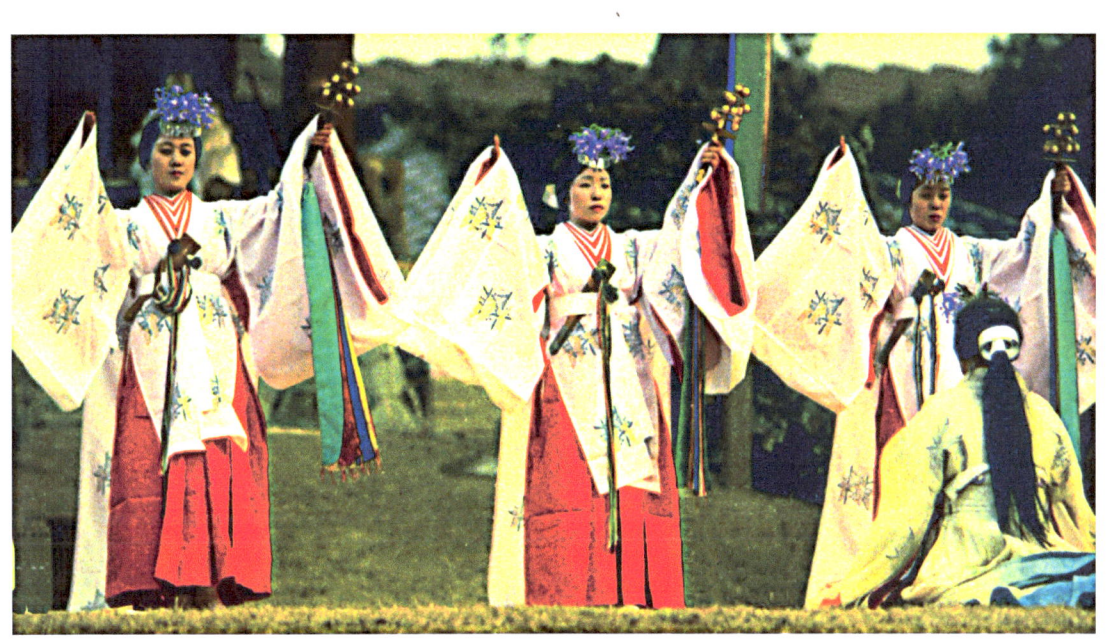

## Pathan Tribesman

North of Peshawar, in the wild Northwest Frontier region of Pakistan, this friendly driver for UNICEF brought us to his home in a remote village.  His wife was furious that their neighbors could see him bringing  foreigners … especially a photographer … into  their mud-walled compound.

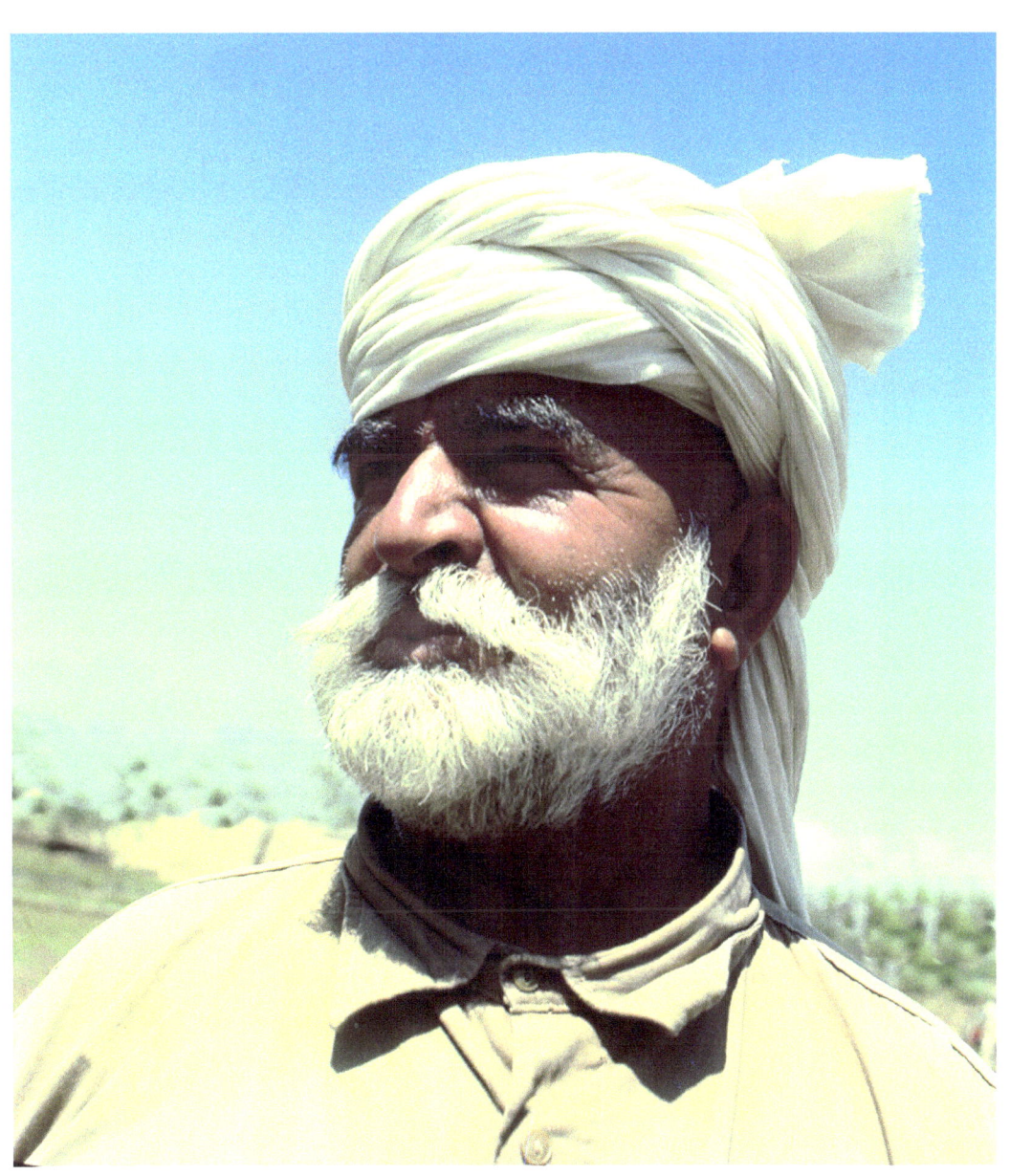

## Nothing Has Changed

For many centuries these Inca … probably even PRE-Inca … terraces have continued to be farmed with skillful irrigation systems, by the Quechua Indians of Peru.  Drawings made centuries ago show farmers with hoes identical to the one this farmer is carrying.  Even his clothes and the designs on them are identical, homespun of llama wool.

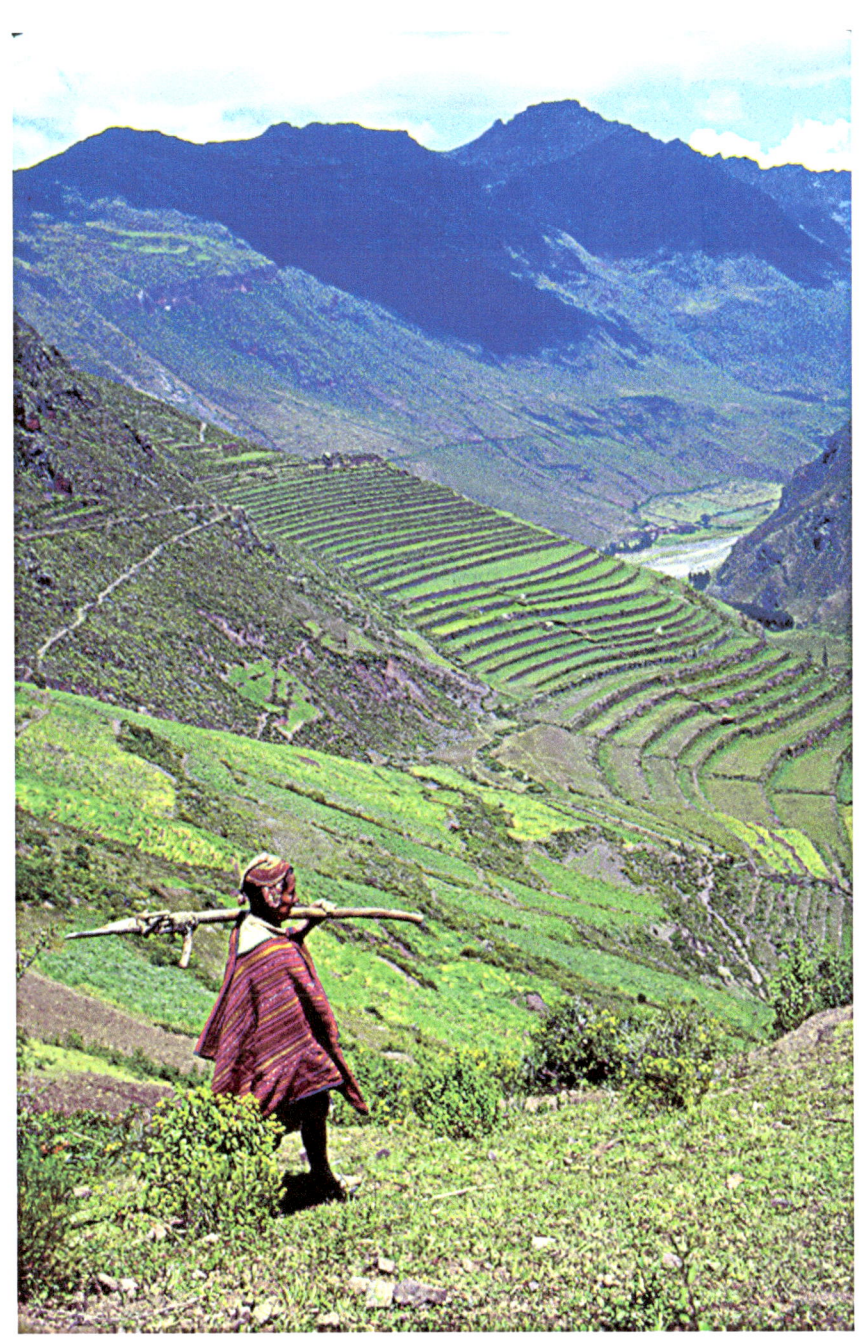

## Life Imitating Art

We usually think of scenic paintings
as being created from life.
But when I saw this bridge, it immediately
reminded me of the famous painting by Whistler
… who had been influenced in this type of
composition by seeing Japanese paintings and
woodblock prints … where only a part of a
subject represents the entire scene, allowing
your mind to imagine the rest.

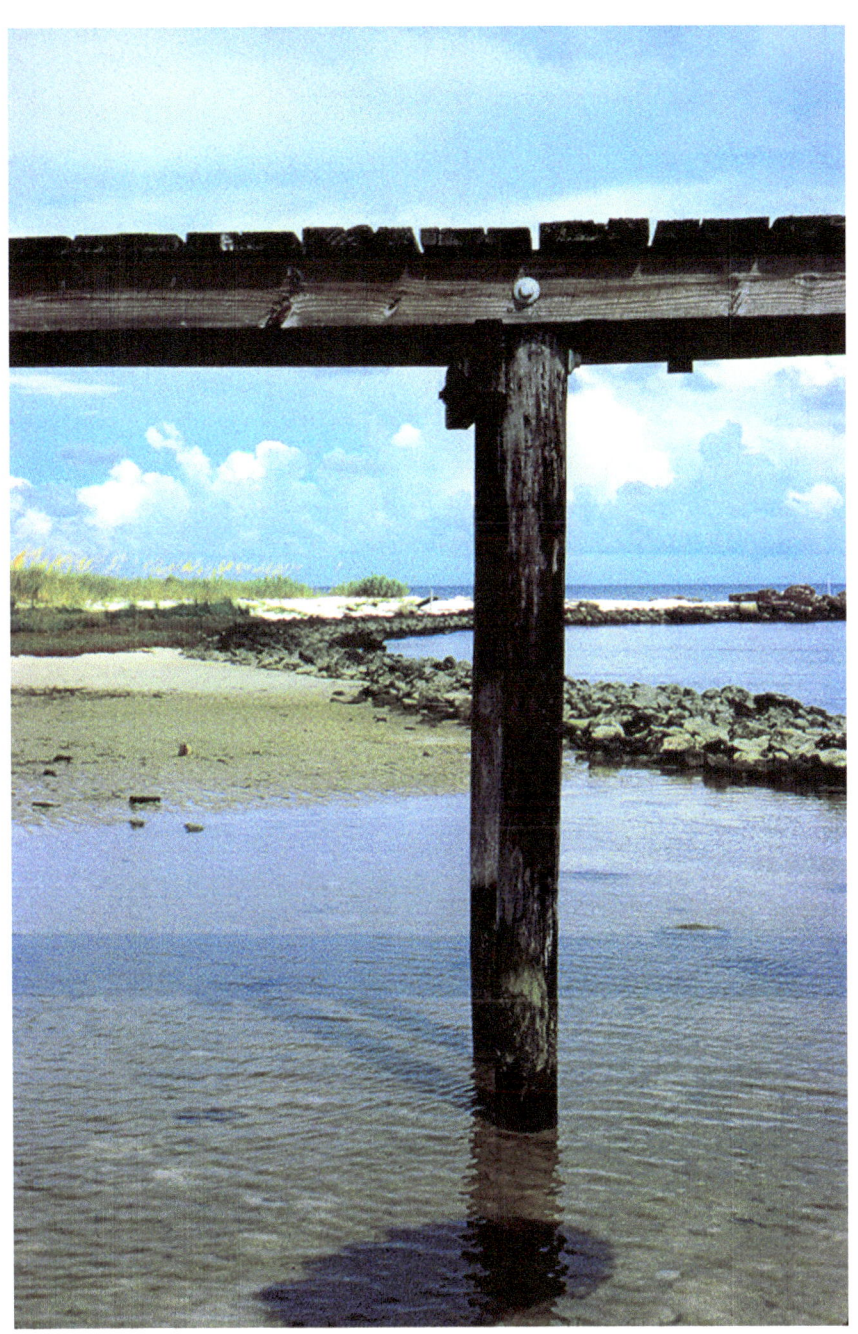

## Reflections

This moonlight, reflecting across the
Pacific … reaching my beach … has
come all the way from the full moon.
Yet it too is only a reflection, reaching
us from the far off Sun

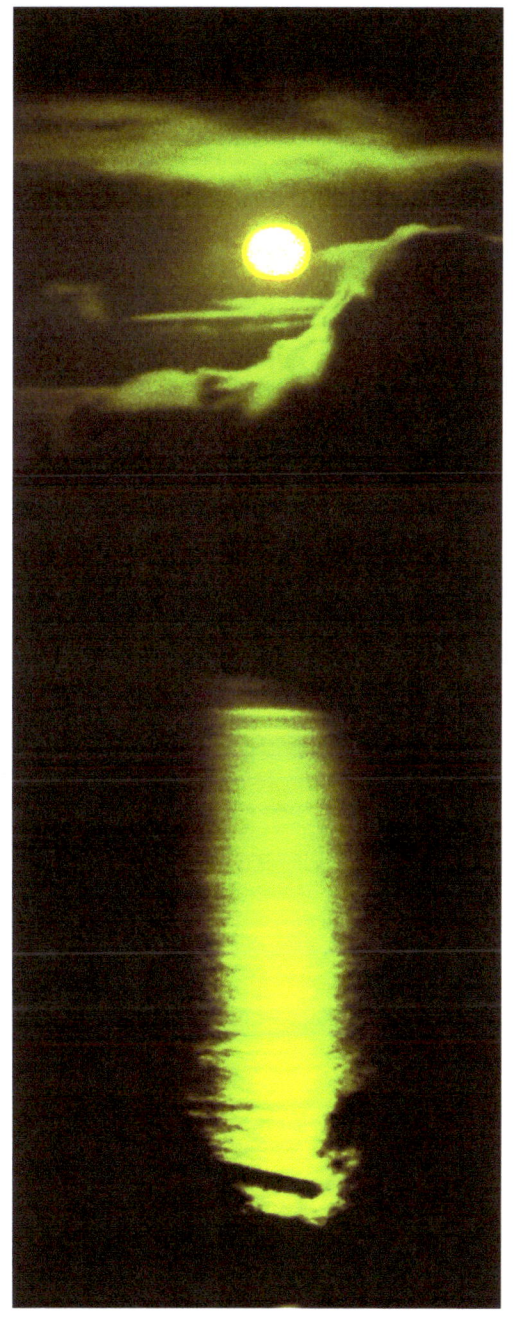

**Cultural Infinity**

**Youth Festival ... aftermath**
**Downtown,  Main St.,  Berlin**

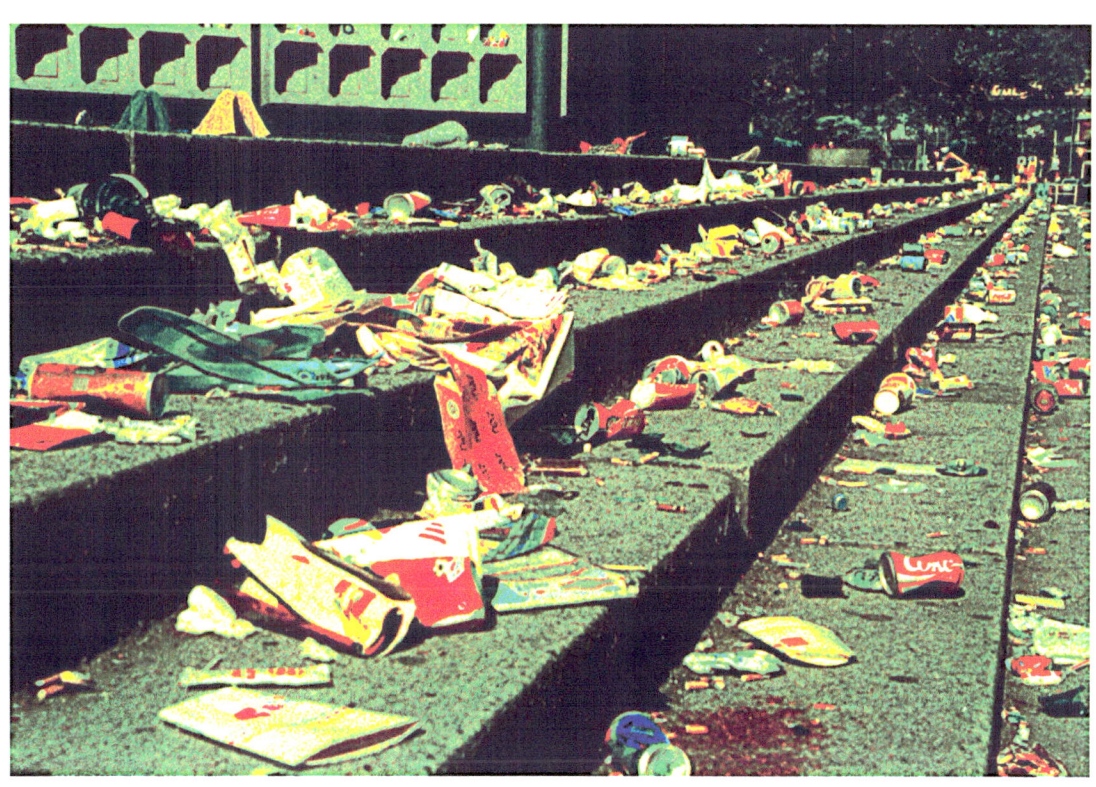

This lovely young lady was a university  student, and a member of the exciting  Bayanihan Philippine Folkloric Dance Group.

Here she wears a traditional Balintawak, with its puffed-up sleeves.  This formal dress, worn  even for weddings, is idea for the warm Philippine climate. The cloth is very light, with an open weave, often made of pineapple fibers.

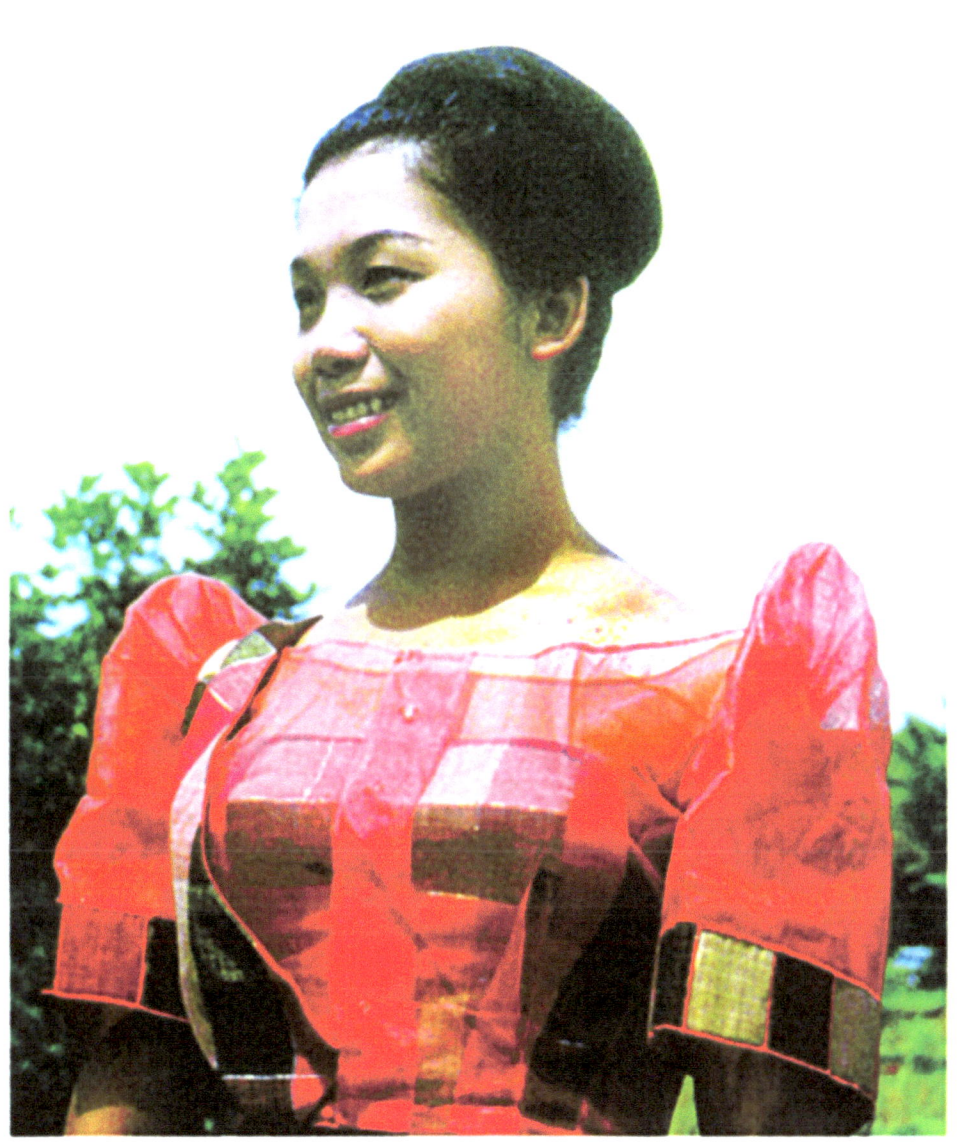

Driving across a vast open plain in central India, the road passed precariously close to this huge boulder … the only one of it's kind anywhere in sight.  Sitting on such a small base, it seemed dangerously liable to topple over, so we sent our strong 3 year old to hold it until we could drive past.

It seems impossible for such a phenomenon to develop, and so isolated on such a flat region.  Yet in my travels I have come across several giant boulders which were even more perfectly shaped, and perched all alone, ready to roll on.

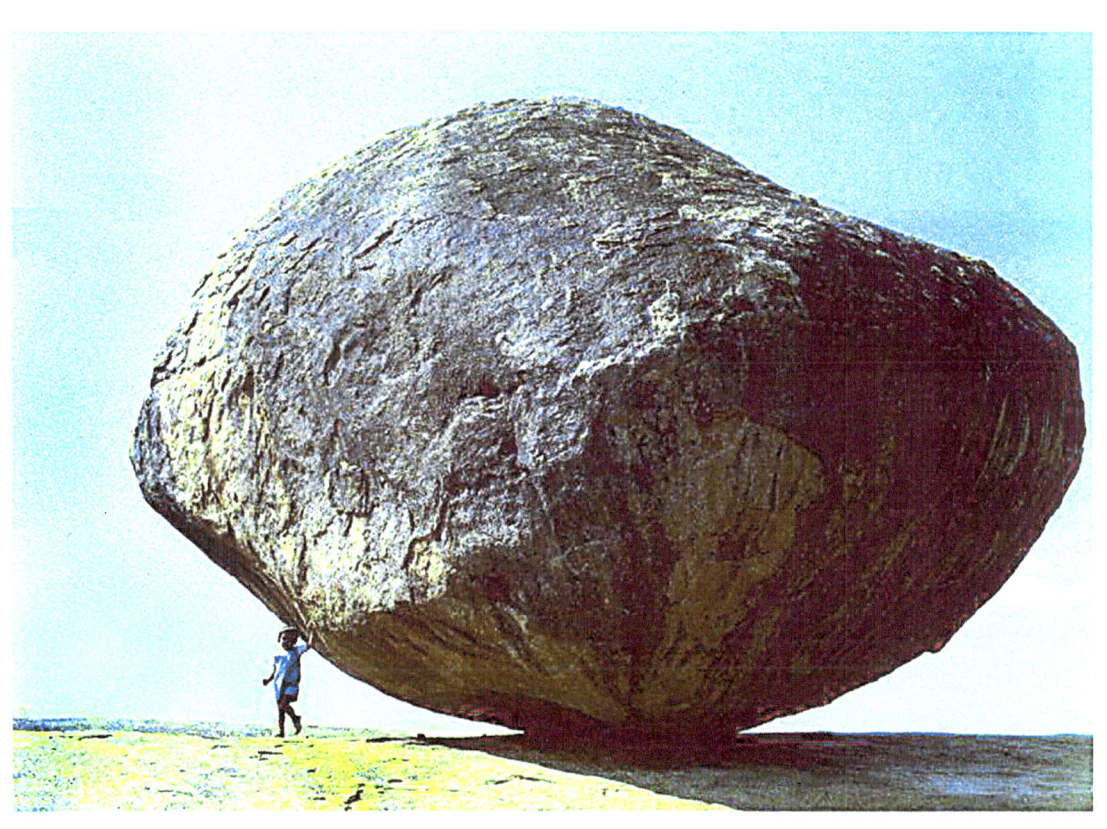

## "Good As Gold"

We hear this often, but how many of us have ANY gold money?

Among the Cuna Indians, living on small islands in the
Caribbean Sea, off the coast of Panama, gold represents the real
wealth of each family.  And of course it's the women who have
... and display ... it.

The Cuna women are most famous for their artistic skills in
creating blouses covered  with designs telling mythological
stories ... some realistic, some symbolic.  To bring out the
designs, they cut through many layers of cloth, using a
reverse appliqué technique, sewing hour after hour, using
extremely fine stiches.

Where do they get the money for gold and the cloth?
By collecting coconuts, which they sell to passing trading
schooners.

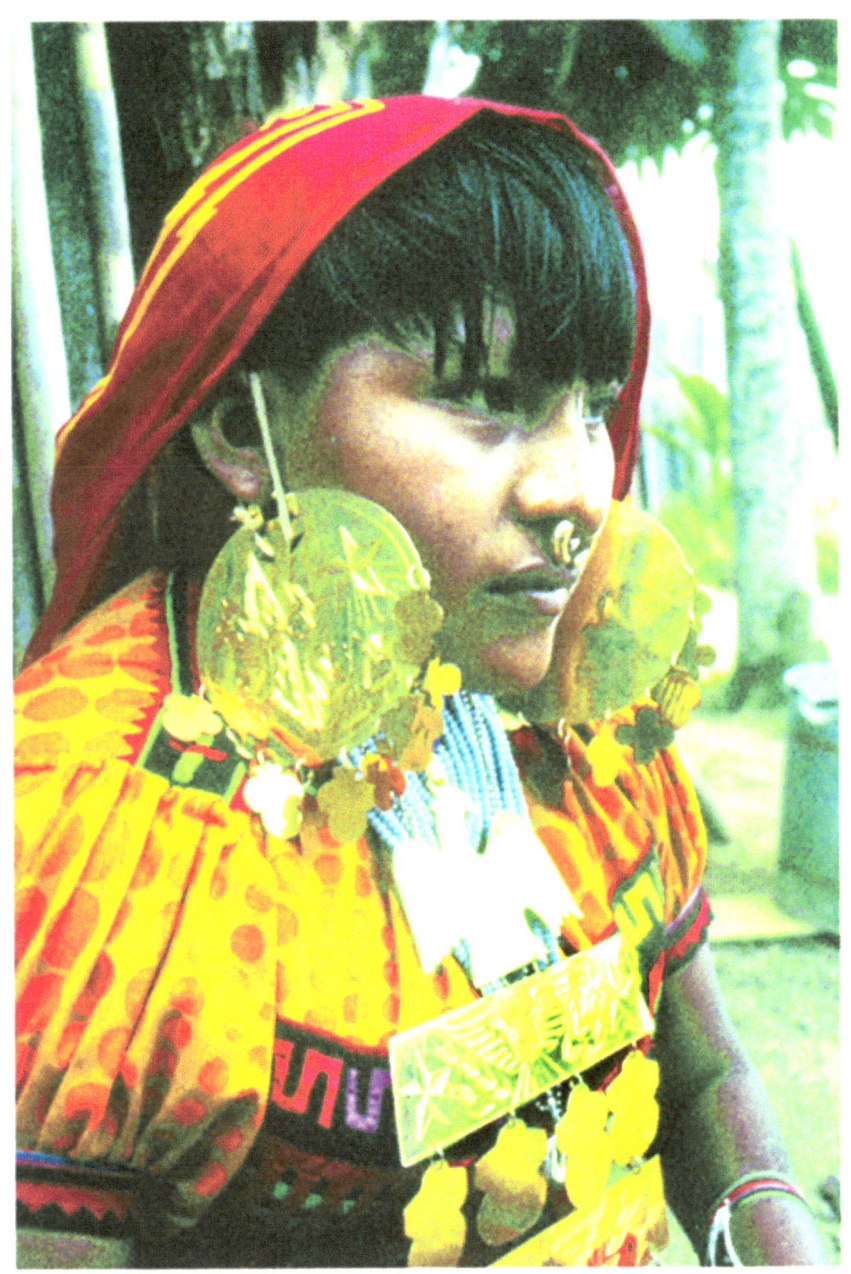

### The Joy Of Life

It seems that every woman of Polynesia loves to
dance. No matter where this woman of Tahiti is,
she goes into dance mode. Add a drum, a guitar
and a bottle of Hinano, and it's party time.

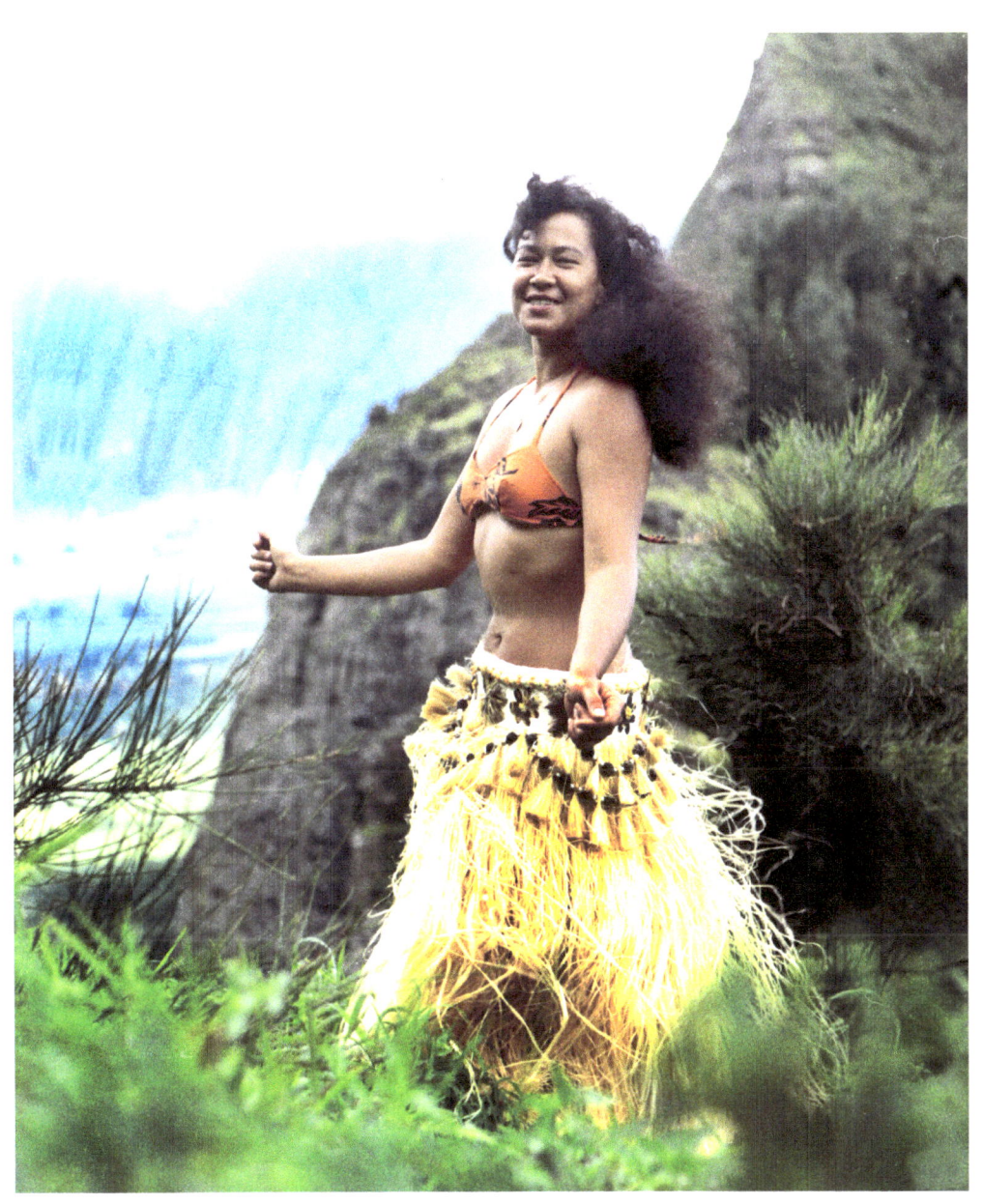

## Sidartha - The BUDDHA

.... whether sculpted in wood, clay, or into rocky cliffs;
painted on silk or rice-paper;  cast in bronze as
miniatures or on gigantic figures reaching to the roof
of temples  ... whether from India, Tibet, China, Thailand,
Afganistan, China or Indonesia ...many words are used
to describe the face of Buddha:  calm, introspective,
composed, passionate, serine, contemplative, or even ...
**BUDDHA-LIKE**

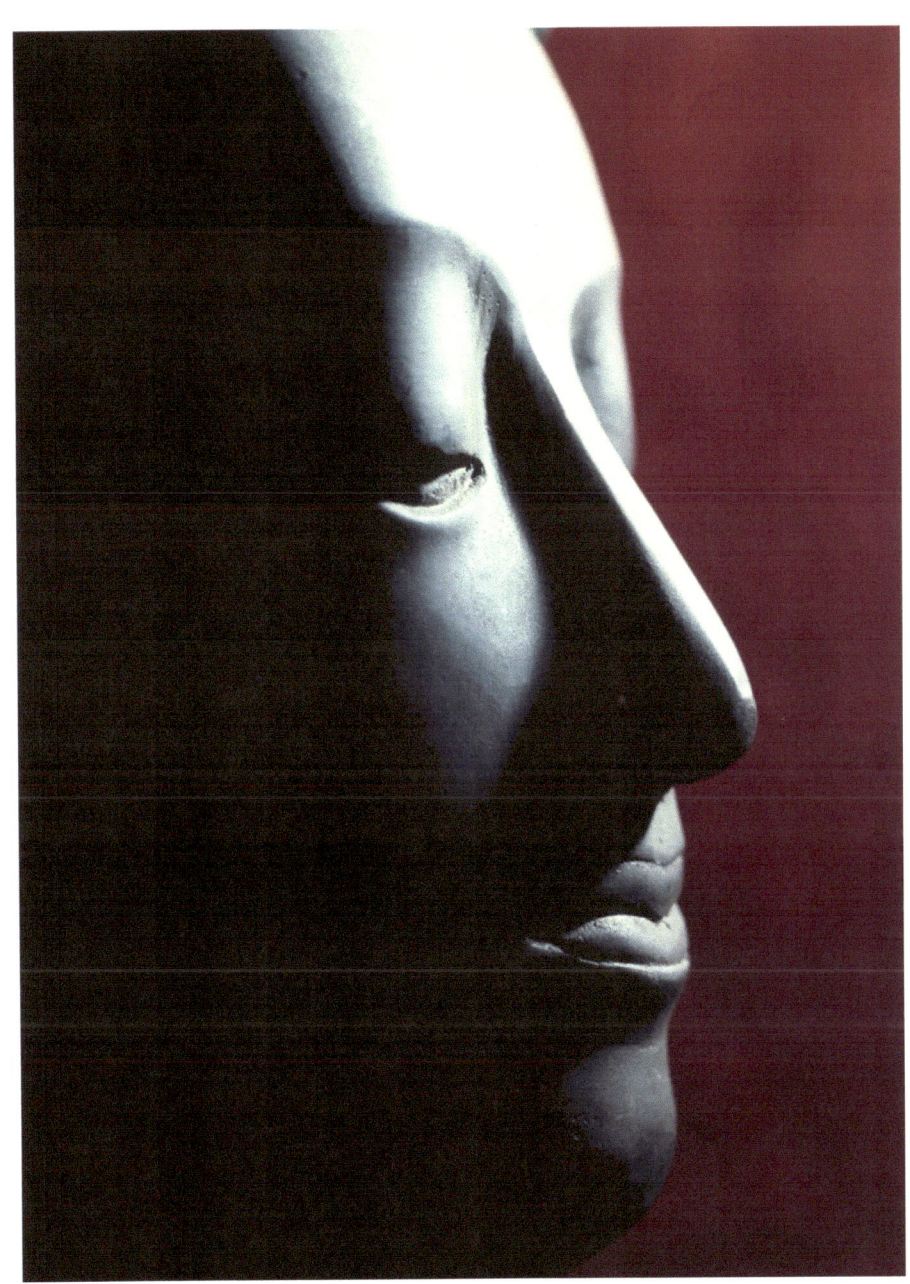

## Pride of The Plains

Every year, summer or autumn, many American Indian
(Amerind) tribes gather for "pow-wows", where they
have competitions of traditional dancers, drummer teams,
horse races and craft artists.

This dancer at the Crow Tribal Fair in Montana, radiates
the feeling that their women have as much strength and
pride in their tribal culture as did their warriors.

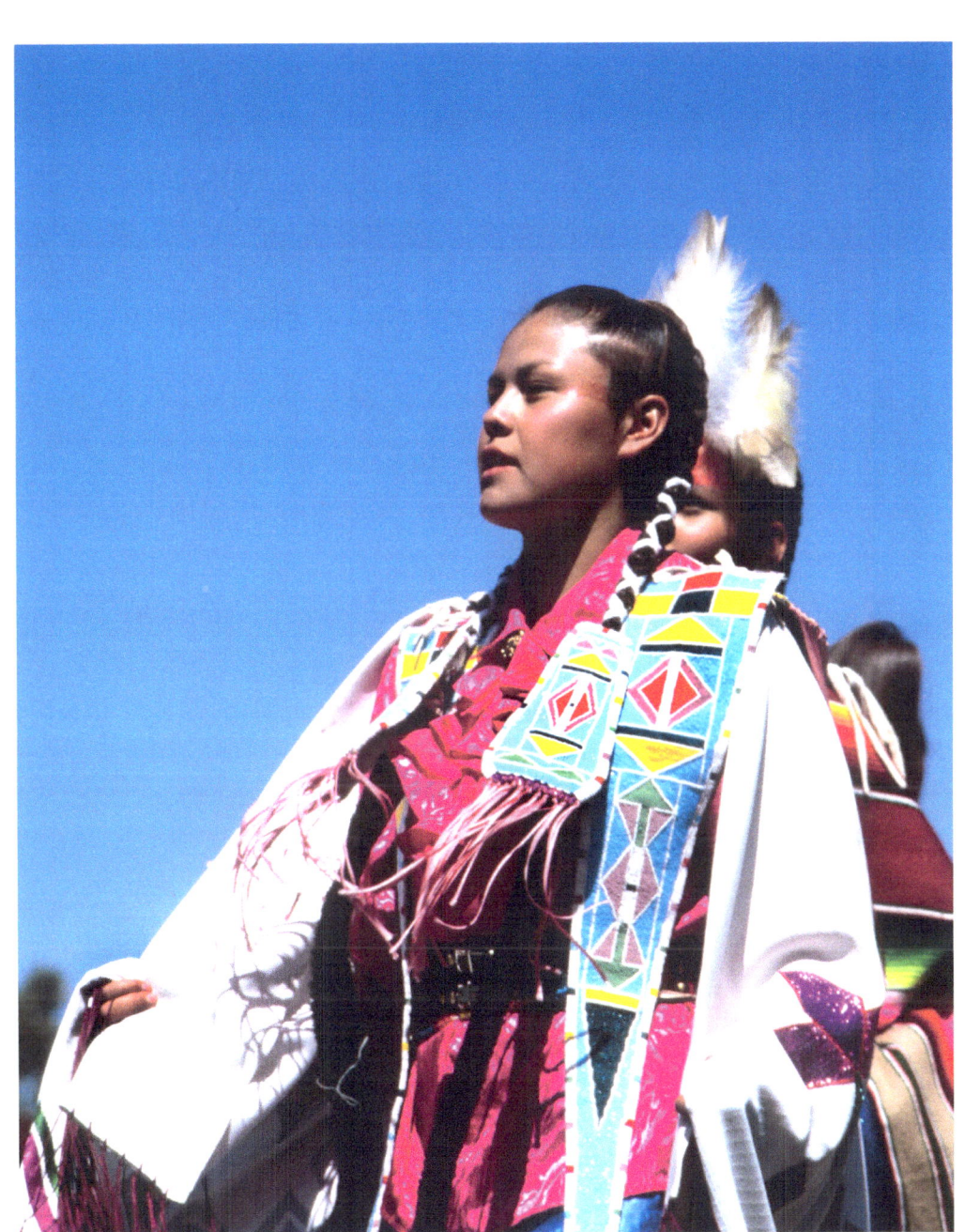

## The Joy of Life  -2

**In Oslo, Norway, there's a park filled with gorgeous sculptures, all of humans, playful, passionate, interwoven …all created by the same artist, Gustav Vigeland.  It was a lifetime project, sponsored by the city.**

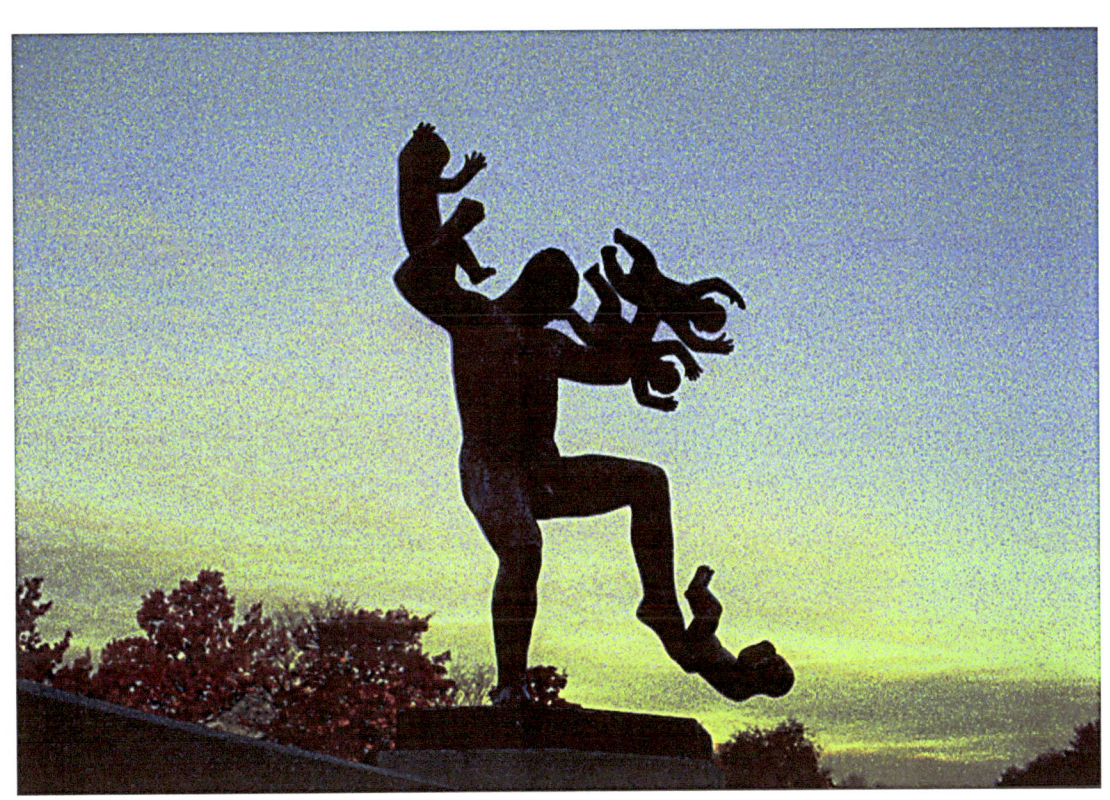

# Author - Photographer

For the past fifty years Wayne Mitchell has been producing curriculum films worldwide, in the field of Social Studies ... filming cultures from Arctic to rainforest, for elementry and secondary students. Over forty of these films are still in distribution (see afana.org/mitchellw.htm ). He was also involved in a few minor occupations such as teaching at Miami University, staff cameraman to J.F. Kennedy, National Park Ranger (Grand Teton & Rocky Mt. Nat. Parks), war correspondent (NBC) in Kashmir and in Viet Nam, Director of Photography for a few feature films in Hollywood, volunteer to UNICEF Children's Fund, story teller ("Tall Tales of the West"), and heavily involved with several Native American Indian tribes. He's now retired from film-making, but busy writing books and magazine articles of his experiences with anthropology, ethnic Art, and tribes around the world.

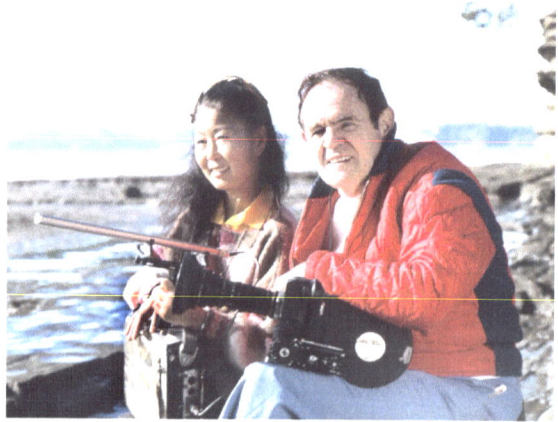

Enlarged prints of the photos in this book, suitable for framing, are available, at reasonable cost. Contact compfilm@clear.net.nz

www.ingramcontent.com/pod-product-compliance
Lightning Source LLC
Chambersburg PA
CBHW051019180526
45172CB00002B/410